GLSEN

Teaching Respect for All

Gay Lesbian Straight Education Network

A resource from the GLSEN lending library

P.O. Box 632747

San Diego, CA 92163

619-226-5786

glsen@aol.com

Women in Love

Portraits of Lesbian Mothers

& Their Families

Women in Love

Portraits of Lesbian Mothers
& Their Families

Photographs & Interviews by Barbara Seyda with Diana Herrera

FOREWORD BY LINDA VILLAROSA

A BULFINCH PRESS BOOK
LITTLE, BROWN AND COMPANY
Boston · New York · Toronto · London

First Edition
ISBN 0-8212-2523-5

Library of Congress Catalog Card Number 97-78358

Bulfinch Press is an imprint and trademark of Little, Brown and Company (Inc.)
Published simultaneously in Canada by Little, Brown & Company (Canada) Limited

Developed and produced by Verve Editions

Designed by Sullivan Scully Design Group

PRINTED IN ITALY

For my grandmother, Mary Seyda, whose creativity inspired me as a child and whose spirit guides me now; my parents, John and Alice Seyda, who taught me to live with integrity, passion and gentleness. And for my precious nephew, Dylan Seyda Tachman (September 29, 1997– October 13, 1997), for the blessings, great lessons and growth he brought to our family. May his soul's journey be with us always.

BARBARA SEYDA

For my grandmother Anastasia, who taught me the power of prayer; my mother Alice, who gave me the gift of life; for Norma Cordell, who taught me the importance of telling my story; Barbara, my life partner who inspired me to journey this dream with her. For all those who expand the love of family to humankind as well as to our Mother Earth. Mitakaye Oyasin. "All My Relations."

DIANA HERRERA

FOREWORD

by Linda Villarosa

I thought I had come out to just about everyone. But since I had my daughter, Kali, a year and a half ago, I've had to start the coming out process all over again. Not long ago, I was faced with the "don't ask, don't tell" dilemma while walking down the street pushing Kali in her stroller. We came upon an older woman who was sitting on her stoop. "What a cutie," she said, looking at Kali and smiling. "Is she yours?" "Yes," I replied, smiling back. So far no problem.

"Hey, I've seen you around," she said, her eyes lighting with recognition. "Don't you live three doors up? You live with the woman who wears the earring in her nose, don't you?"

This was the proverbial moment of truth, and I was faced with a couple of choices. Telling an outright lie such as "Yes, she's my roommate," didn't cross my mind, since I never again will lie about my sexuality. I had done enough of that during my long coming out process which started in college and had ended — I thought — when I came out in print in *Essence*, the magazine I used to work for, in 1993. But if I said, "Yes — gotta run now," she could assume that my nose-ring-wearing lover and co-parent, Vickie, was a friend or tenant, and that she'd hear more about my husband another time.

At that moment I felt all of the dread that every lesbian or gay person feels each time we are faced with this kind of coming out decision: Do I take the easy (and chicken) route and let myself "pass" as hetero-sexual, taking advantage of my new baby as a perfect prop? Or do I come out and face the uneasy possibility of rejection — which in this case could also mean a rejection of Kali. How would it feel to have this neighbor disapprove of my daughter? And would she rally other neighbors on the block against us?

For me, the idea of becoming a mother was as natural as taking a breath. I love my own mother fiercely and cherish the close relationship we've carved out after several years of struggle over my lesbianism. A successful — and aggressive — businesswoman whom my friends sometimes refer to as "The Enforcer," my mother has always spoken glowingly about motherhood; she once told me that raising my sister and me was the most important, rewarding work of her life.

I was lucky to find in Vickie a life partner who shared my passion for parenthood. We eventually decided that I would get pregnant, because I was older and my biological clock seemed to be ticking loudly enough to be heard in neighboring states. Because I have a very close relationship with my father, it was important for me that we use a known donor, so that our baby could know her or his father. We recruited a close gay friend, Lorry, who had always wanted children but wasn't interested in taking on all of the responsibility.

With our plans in place, we set about trying to "make" our baby. When the time was right (according to my temperature, a chart I'd been keeping for six months and an ovulation testing kit), Lorry came over, went into the spare bedroom, and emerged five minutes later with some sperm in a cup. Vickie helped, using a syringe and a speculum to insert the sperm into my body. Three weeks later, as I found myself retching over my garbage can at work, I wondered if this experiment might have actually worked. Did we really create a child? The morning I saw the dark blue line on the home pregnancy test was just about the happiest moment of my life.

Telling people that I was pregnant was an interesting — often hilarious — process. I loved to watch people struggle with a range of expressions — shock, confusion, throat-clearing and finally genuine joy and good feelings. My favorite question, clearly from someone who hadn't been paying close attention during that little talk about the birds and the bees in sixth grade science class: "Is Vickie the, uhhh, father?" Someone else wondered if the most planned, discussed, obsessed-over decision of our lives was "an accident," and if we had "really thought about the consequences" of what we were doing.

Despite recent publicity (including a Melissa Ethridge-Julie Cypher *Newsweek* cover), lesbian baby-making is pretty much of an unknown entity. Watching me walking, or rather waddling down the street with my bulging belly, I'm sure it was easier for people to believe that I was the virgin Mary than a pregnant lesbian. To most people, the word lesbian couldn't possibly describe someone who's also a mother. (In fact, a few years ago, the idea seemed so ridiculous to a judge in Florida that he awarded custody of a 10-year-old girl to her father — a convicted murderer — over her lesbian mother.)

During the months that followed as I got bigger and bigger and bigger, I rarely thought "Hey, I'm a pregnant lesbian." I was too busy trying to get through my day on only one nap and one stealth trip to McDonalds. And during labor with my mother holding one leg and Vickie holding the other, I certainly wasn't thinking, "I'm a lesbian having a baby." I was too busy trying to push my daughter into the world. And now that Kali is here, I never think, "I'm a lesbian mother." I'm just a mom like billions of others. When I'm watching nervously as she tries to drag herself and a toy or two up the steps, there's no difference. When she wakes up and yells "Mom, mom, up" and I can't wait to give her a morning hug, there's no difference. When I look down at her while she's sitting on my lap "reading" a book to me and her well-worn doll, there's no difference.

But in other ways besides the conception, our experience is radically different. When I listen to my heterosexual friends complain that they never get out, I breathe a sigh of relief that we have a committed network of lesbian and gay friends — our chosen family — many of whom do not have their own children, and who love our daughter almost as if she were their own. Vickie and I feel comfortable leaving Kali with any of them while we spend some time alone together to keep ourselves sane as still-new moms.

Even more immediate, Kali has three parents. Period. That's how it is, and that's how we'll explain it to her when the time comes. Her daddy loves her just as much as her two moms love her, and it makes no difference in our daily routines that we have varying degrees of genetic and legal attachments to each other.

Thinking about Kali and all of the people in her life, I was finally able to do the right thing that day with my neighbor. If I were to allow her to think that Vickie was just my roommate, I'd be denying the reality of our family. That would erase all the nights Vickie has shaken off sleep to bring me the baby to nurse, blunt the tears of joy she shed in the delivery room when Kali's head first appeared between my legs and cancel out her face as she gazes at our baby with so much love and hope.

So I answered, "The woman with the nose ring is the baby's other mother." And, without missing a beat, our neighbor replied "Oh, you're lesbians, isn't that nice." And she turned to the baby and said, "Aren't you lucky to have two mommies who love you so much."

INTRODUCTION
by Barbara Seyda

THE PROJECT *Women in Love* began in 1993 as a small seed inside a country farmhouse in New Mexico. It was Thanksgiving and Diana and I were sitting in old rocking chairs watching the evening unfurl like a post-Modern Norman Rockwell painting: the background music was Hip Hop, the children were a patchwork quilt of radiant faces from around the world and the women setting the table were all lesbian mothers.

We sat and watched the children spread like confetti throughout the house. Their skin was the color of ochre, cinnamon, sienna and sand. They were from

India, Guatemala, Mexico and the U.S. and most of them had been adopted. Some wore blinking high-tops; others wore rollerblades, Chicago Bulls caps and hid "glo-in-the-dark" rocks in their baggy pants pockets. They told us jokes and ran

through the house — a mandala of giggles. Their mothers were in the kitchen basting a 20 lb. turkey and returning it to the oven, removing foil from baked sweet potatoes and setting out apple and pear pies. That evening I knew we must document the stories of the families gathered there. I knew the confluence of lives, developmental changes, discoveries and struggles of these families were not considered significant by the mainstream media, but needed to be recorded and valued historically.

In December of 1993, I went to the editorial offices of *Mothering* magazine in Santa Fe and secured an assignment — a feature on lesbian mothers. Diana offered to assist me and we interviewed 10 mothers and 15 children in New Mexico. I submitted 26 black and white photographs (some of which are in this book) and a 5,000 word story with two sidebars. Within three weeks, the editors at *Mothering* refused to consider the story for publication. They sent me a $75 kill fee and a few comments about how they liked the photographs, but the story lacked angst and drama. For the next year, I submitted the story and photographs to other mainstream publications such as *Parenting, Family Circle, Family Life, Redbook* and *Ladies' Home Journal* and received homophobic editorial feedback and no interest in publication.

By the summer of 1995, I was feeling frustrated about the impossibility of placing the story anywhere. In August, a friend of Diana's came to visit from Oregon. She took one look at the photos collecting dust on my desk and said, "You have to do a book. Lesbians would love a book like this." That fall, I took her advice and wrote an 18 page book proposal and sent it to agents and publishers in New York. I received what seemed like an endless series of rejection letters. No one was interested in the subject or could visualize a market for this work. Apparently, the millions of lesbian mothers living in the U.S. today were not considered a "viable market" and no one was willing to take a risk on such a great unknown.

At the time, Diana was supporting us through her acupuncture practice and we discussed raising the money ourselves, but it seemed an insurmountable task.

What we had to launch this project was humble: a $250 check from my parents to cover postage and copying costs, an old beat-up Honda, a tape recorder, my Canon and a pile of notebooks. Somehow, perhaps through divine inspiration, by December of 1995, we decided to embark on our first grassroots fundraising campaign and began traveling to meet with women philanthropists and anyone who could donate or invest an amount, however great or small. Our fundraising efforts culminated this year with a grand total of $85,000, which came in through the years in spurts and trickles. Many times, we had to cancel trips due to lack of funds, or film sat at the lab for months because we couldn't pay the bill. We never had a computer until the very end of the project, when the advance came through from our publisher, Bulfinch Press. All of the interviews were transcribed by hand by Diana, and I sat at Kinko's or the library putting the manuscript on disk.

The composite for this project passed through many hands and fortunately ended up with Gary Chassman of Verve Editions in 1996. Gary provided the critical link to Carol Judy Leslie of Bulfinch Press nine months later. Without the vision and dedication of Verve Editions and Bulfinch Press, we would still be on the road continuing to raise money. What sustained us through the long stretches when there were just a few cents in the project account was the experience of meeting the families. While we were traveling to raise funds, we photographed and interviewed mothers and grandmothers from all walks of life. Their voices carried us to unforgettable places. Listening to their stories, told from the heart, was what sustained us on our journey. This book is filled with their faces and their lives.

THE STATISTICS There are an estimated 10 million lesbian mothers living in the U.S. today, and that number is increasing each day. In 1995, the American Psychological Association published a definitive compilation of research on lesbian and gay parents in order to provide assistance to parents, lawyers, teachers, clinicians, researchers, psychologists, students and those involved in legal and policy issues related to lesbian and gay parenting. They state: "In summary, there is no evidence to suggest that lesbians and gay men are unfit to be parents or that the psychosocial development among children of lesbian or gay parents is compromised in any respect, relative to the offspring of heterosexual parents. Not a single study has found children of gay or lesbian parents to be disadvantaged in any significant respect relative to children of heterosexual parents. The evidence to date suggests that home environments provided by lesbian and gay parents are as likely as those provided by heterosexual parents to support and enable children's psychosocial growth."

Accurate information, such as this summary of research, has been available for years — along with references, annotated bibliographies, empirical studies, articles, books and additional resources. In spite of the existence of comprehensive studies, widespread stereotypes and beliefs about lesbian mothers persist. We hope that this book disrupts those long-held and misinformed assumptions.

What has struck us traveling across the country and meeting so many lesbian mothers is a sense of the complexity and richness of their lives — of the multi-faceted spectrum of lesbian motherhood.

No one can say "lesbian mother" and mean something specific, because any one woman with a child is defined by a myriad of experiences and circumstances, intersecting economics, ethnic and cultural heritage, spiritual or religious beliefs, sexual perspective and expression. What affects her and influences her life can be the stories her grandmother told her, childhood sexual abuse, how much income she earns or who she is financially dependent upon, what is expected of her by her family, what she expects of herself, how she is connected to the father or donor of her child, her desire to care for a child from another part of the world, how she was mothered herself, her connection to her own body and her ability to accept the unknown.

After completing this project, what is evident is the immense and untapped wisdom, insight, love and compassion of these women. We are challenged to grow through listening to their stories. Only then can we begin to see what connects us and what prevents us from understanding the truth of each other's lives.

What shines strongly through these interviews and portraits is that these lesbians — these women — are *mothers*. Regardless of their sexuality, or whether their children came to them through intercourse, insemination with known or unknown sperm donors, or formal or informal adoption, these mothers are the nurturers of life. Their concerns are the same as those of all mothers: keeping their children safe, helping them to grow, maintaining relationships, juggling demands on time, discovering limits and boundaries, hoping and working for a peaceful world. The sooner society sees that fact and recognizes that it is primary, the sooner prejudice against lesbian mothers will dissipate.

MY GRANDFATHER'S PORTRAIT When Diana and I were halfway through this project, I was talking to my mom on the phone one day. My mother is one of nine children and was born and raised in Hammond, Indiana. Her father, Martin Kowalik, a Polish immigrant whom she barely knew, died when she was six years old. I said, "Mom, do you have any pictures of your father? Do you remember what he looked like?" She said, "No. We never owned a camera. Grandma ran the grocery store to support us and there was no money to buy a camera. It was something we couldn't afford." I was stunned. Her words fell with a jolt of finality.

In this age, we are overwelmed with reproduced images and cheap cameras bought at Walgreens, bus kiosks with larger-than-life Herb Ritts photos, slick pseudo-porn fashion magazine layouts, newspaper images of international atrocity and local violence. Yet my mother doesn't have a picture of her father. This single fact created a huge silence within me.

This realization underscored the necessity of continuing to photograph and document the intimate moments within families, especially those moments of warmth, beauty, courage and triumph often censored, devalued, or simply overlooked by the mainstream media.

AN INVOCATION We thank all of the women and children who shared their lives with us, because there were many who couldn't. Hundreds of lesbian mothers lose their children every year because sexual orientation is used as an issue to decide custody. In most parts of the United States, lesbians still face the serious threat of losing their children if they end up in court. Because of societal and judicial prejudice, every lesbian mother can feel an overwelming vulnerability few heterosexual parents ever confront. Also, we are currently witnessing a rise of custody battles between lesbian women who have separated or divorced since forming their families.

In most parts of the U.S., non-biological mothers are denied any power, authority and rights to make decisions concerning their children. Legislative changes need to be made responding to the reality of our families, to protect the future of the children involved and the rights of all mothers.

These photographs and stories are the umbilical cords that connect us to each other. Through them, may we trace the infinite contours of the human heart.

REBECCA DiNINO AND GAYLE CHILDERS
New York

At 6:30 a.m., Gayle Childers was walking her dogs, "Autumn" and "Licorice," in a quiet Brooklyn neighborhood. We arrived just before sunrise, when the air was still cool and the sky was a deep urban grey. Dressed in a sharp, sage-colored suit, Gayle was heading to a meeting on Wall Street that morning, and her partner Rebecca, eight months pregnant, was still working full-time as a child psychoanalyst for a hospital in White Plains. We went into their backyard for photos as the sun rose and their faces lit up with all the great anticipation and exuberance of expectant motherhood.

Gayle: We both played softball in the same Brooklyn league in Prospect Park, but we were on different teams. The first memory I have of Rebecca was at a party thrown after the Bombers won the championship in 1988. Remember that Bec?

Rebecca: Oh, completely. Our team was knocked out instantly in the playoffs. I was there with a friend of mine watching the rest of the games. She is a "you-have-to-be-dating" kind of person and said, "Let's find somebody for you." It sounds silly now, but I said, "Oh, look at her. She's really cute." And it was Gayle. That night at the championship party, I threw myself at her.

Gayle: Rebecca was all over me. It wasn't subtle at all. Once we started going out, that was it. But it took us a long time to get to where we are now. Contrary to what I consider to be the beginning of a typical relationship where everything is "peachy and wonderful"— that unrealistic phase is something we didn't have. It was actually very hard.

Rebecca: Our friends didn't think we'd make it through the first two years. We seemed to be fighting all the time. We had a lot of work and negotiation to do. It took a long time, but eventually we had a life together that we both really enjoyed and asked, "What can we do to make our lives fuller?"

Gayle: We talked about having children for several years. The deciding factors were we wanted children and we wanted our children to be representative of both of us. We selected an African-American donor who was tall, because my family's tall.

Rebecca: In our society, bi-racial children are considered black. If I gave birth, I knew people might not think they were my children. They would assume they were Gayle's children. Also I knew a lot of bi-racial adult women and almost all of them went through a phase of hating their white mothers. I thought that would be devastating to go through with my kids.

Another issue for me was the idea of not working and depending on someone financially. The women in my family were breadwinners. They were the ones the family depended on economically. My aunt, cousins and my mom always worked. I have always worked, but we've had to incrementally combine our incomes. Eventually I knew Gayle and I had built a secure foundation based on trust and we would go through whatever we needed to go through as a family.

> "We talked about having children for several years. The deciding factors were we wanted children and we wanted our children to be representative of both of us."

Gayle: When Rebecca missed her period and went to the doctor, they did a sonogram and said, "There's one. No, there's two!" We had always talked about having two kids, so it was a godsend to happen at once.

Rebecca: The first three months I was sick off and on. I was nauseated and eating little pieces of bread 24 hours a day. The next three months were really good.

Gayle: At four months, we had an amniocentesis and found out they were boys.

Rebecca: Once we knew they were boys, we decided to pick their names. "Caleb" is a name I really liked and "James" is a name I also liked and it's my father's name, so we chose "Caleb James."

Gayle: I liked "Colin" and "Patrick" is my grandfather's middle name, so we decided on "Colin Patrick."

Rebecca: One of the most fascinating things about being pregnant is the developing babies. As we speak, Caleb has the hiccups. Now they move around all the time. I can feel their heads. It's just a thrill. Caleb is on the left side low and Colin is transverse across the top. I don't know if this happens to all pregnant women, but since I've been pregnant, I've sort of lost my memory. Sometimes, I can't remember things from day-to-day. My best friend will walk up to me and I can't remember her name. Or at times, I couldn't remember why I wanted to have children. I try to remember all the conversations Gayle and I had.

I've talked to other women with young children and they say they felt the same thing, like, "I can't believe I did this!"

Gayle: Our entire lives are about to change as these new beings come into our lives. What I want to instill in my sons foremost is having integrity and strength of character. And making sure they have role models who are positive male figures. I want to be there emotionally for them and be able to play with them, give them a good education and bring them up to believe in themselves. This is our family and integrity, love and giving will define it.

I'm happy that my dad lives in New York and has been very supportive. He will be very involved with his grandsons. We've also received a lot of support from our lesbian friends. For my mother and my sister, it took quite a bit for them to come to grips with this. They would say, "We live with the fact that you're a dyke. And you have a white partner. Okay, we're dealing with that." Then Rebecca and I got married and had a ceremony and now we're having children. For them, we keep going one step further, which is hard for them to get used to. But this is our family and I can't hide it.

Rebecca's picture is on my desk at work. I thought it was important to let the people I work directly with know we were having a family, so I told my team one day. They were silent and dumbfounded when I said it. Then they asked some questions. Now people who I've worked with for years ask me how Rebecca is doing. That's a really good feeling.

> "Our entire lives are about to change as these new beings come into our lives."

We drove down a dirt road to an A-frame house with green trim and an iris garden. It was thundering and about to rain when we arrived at Cal and Mo's three acres between the Sandia and the Sangre de Cristo Mountains. Born in Detroit in 1962, Mo is a pediatric occupational therapist of Irish/English descent. Cal was born in Seattle in 1952 and is associate director of the autism program at the University of New Mexico. They have two daughters — Hallie (4), conceived through insemination, and Azucena (1), adopted from Guatemala — a golden retriever called "Champ," a white dog, "Tajar," and "Debro" the cat. Painted footprints on paper hung on the living room wall with two marionettes from Burma. Hallie wore light blue pumps and a gold tiara and Azucena ate crackers and gurgled during the interview.

Mo: I have always wanted to give birth to a child. I thought it was such a miracle, so when we decided to have a baby, we interviewed everybody we knew with our tablet of questions.

Cal: I'm the kind of person who has to know everything.

Mo: We interviewed people who adopted, people who chose not to have children, people who had older kids, people with babies, people who knew the sperm donor and those who didn't. It took a long time, but we did a whole lot of mental and spiritual preparation. The first time we inseminated, I got pregnant with Hallie. But I felt like we worked on it for so long.

Cal: We talked about having more than one child. Mo would like to have seven or eight probably. Two or three was where we came to an agreement. After having Hallie, Mo tried to get pregnant again with the same sperm, but after nine months, she couldn't get pregnant.

By that time, we were researching adoption. We had always planned to adopt one of our children. We felt really strongly about adopting in Guatemala because we felt pretty connected to the people up in the hills, the Mayan people. We knew we wanted a baby from Guatemala who was of Mayan descent.

Mo: We also felt socially conscious about bringing children into the world and how much our earth can support. We knew there were children in the world today who could use a home. So I called up an agency here and said, "Hi. My name is Mo Taylor. I'm a lesbian and our family wants to adopt a child." They said, "It's not a problem." They recommended that one parent adopt, bring the child back to the States and then do the second adoption.

Cal: Later, we almost didn't get Azucena. The Guatemalan Council had stopped the adoption process at the very end. Two weeks before we were to go down and pick our daughter up, they called the adoption agency and said they knew two women were waiting to adopt and that was not okay. The adoption agency said, "We know these people. They are loving, caring parents of

"**We also felt socially conscious about bringing children into the world and how much our earth can support.**"

another child. There's no reason not to allow this adoption through." We had to get more reference letters and letters of support sent down, and then they granted the adoption.

Mo: What it boiled down to was that we went down as a family to pick Azucena up. They wanted Cal to go down alone and bring her home. We said, "No, Hallie is not going to think that her sister dropped out of an airplane and I don't want to be left out." We were adamant about going down as a family.

Cal: In the end, we were introduced as godmother and mother. We saw Azu's foster family quite a bit after we got her because we wanted a peaceful transition for her. We talked to them every night because we'd say, "Azu's crying and pulling on her ear. Do you think she has an earache?" and they'd say, "No, she pulls on her ear when she's uncomfortable."

Mo: We told Hallie what was happening all along, even when they weren't going to sign the papers. We explained that because our family is different, other people might not let Azucena come home with us. She was silent after that. But when we were on the plane, she stood on her seat and said to the three rows behind us, "I'm a teacher and I'm teaching you about my family. I have two moms and that's okay. It's good to have two moms. And I'm going to get my sister!"

Just by verbalizing your life, you affect people. Very few people would have thought that Azu might not be able to come home with us because we are lesbians. It affected our friends and family in a very profound way. It was hitting home and hurting them.

Cal: We are more on the quiet side, but we feel the need to lead our lives truthfully and openly.

Mo: Now, we're going through the second-parent adoption with Azu. We feel we need the legal rights to our children for the kids' sake. We were concerned when Cal adopted Hallie because you have no choice of judges. There are certain judges in the state who will allow two women to adopt and some who won't. We were given to a criminal justice judge who our lawyer thought would pass it. It was pretty emotional to be sitting in the courtroom with your baby and just wanting to be a family and then a whole string of criminals with their chains around their ankles walk through. And you're all in the same courtroom with each other. And they could have shot somebody's mother for all we know.

Cal: The judge ended up being really nice and was so pleased to do our adoption.

Mo: I think parenting is the biggest responsibility you can have in the world. The way we're going to help the world is to raise children that will help make this world a loving and caring place.

MIKI AND MICHAEL ADACHI
California

We arrived at Miki Adachi's home in a Bay Area suburb on a quiet Sunday morning. Miki is a 44-year-old third-generation Japanese-American Buddhist logistics supervisor and single mom. She greeted us wearing a tie-dyed T-shirt and holding Michael and his orange tiger. Just a little over a year old, Michael sat proudly in his Mickey Mouse chair and played his drum after the interview ended.

I actually can't give you a good reason why I decided to have a child. I just wanted a companion, someone to teach me what love is all about and show me what discovery and learning are. I think I was numb and bored with life, so I wanted to bring those qualities out in myself.

Finally when I hit 40, my doctor said, "Look, go see a counselor and talk about it." I did and we talked about all the things that stopped me from going forward with getting pregnant. I realized all the things you worry about, like a college fund, are years down the road. Being single and being a lesbian, you wonder if it's unfair for the child and why would you want to subject a human being to those conditions. We discussed if the child would develop irregularly or abnormally without a father.

It took me about a year to get pregnant. I inseminated 11 times. When I was 42, Michael was born.

I picked a sperm bank that had a lot of Asian donors, meaning one page worth, which is more than all the others. I picked someone who had characteristics I liked, that complemented my own, such as creativity and spontaneity. The donor wrote that he was gregarious and musical. The donor is about 5'10" and in my family, the tallest male is 5'4". He was a Chinese donor, so Michael is half-Chinese and half-Japanese.

When I told my mom that I was pregnant, her reaction was shock. She said, "Miki, why couldn't you go out and find a nice man?" She didn't talk about it to her sisters or to my dad. My dad's 83 now. When I told him, he said nothing — nothing, that's why I thought he didn't hear me the first time. My mother finally warmed up to the idea and could express happiness when we had the baby shower when I was eight months pregnant. Ever since then, she's been wonderful.

My wish for Michael is for him to be able to show love and affection. I think it's partially cultural that my parents and I don't touch each other. We don't hug. We don't show affection. So I definitely want to change that this time around.

My responsibility as a parent is to help him love himself. That's the most important, not necessarily the easiest. Sometimes I forget he really doesn't care what toys or clothes he has. It doesn't have to be the Baby Gap or Oshkosh. He doesn't care.

If I can somehow show him that I love myself and I'm proud of being a lesbian, then hopefully he'll grow up thinking positively about himself. My greatest challenge is loving myself.

I have imagined a world where all mothers are respected and treated equally, to be judged only by their skills as mothers. I hope someday it won't even be necessary to do a book on what it's like being a lesbian mom. I am a mother. I'm not as different as you think.

> "If I can somehow show him that I love myself and I'm proud of being a lesbian, then he'll grow up thinking positively about himself. My greatest challenge is loving myself."

*L*isa Bibbens and Pam Liberty live in a Santa Fe-style adobe out in the desert with their two-year-old daughter, McKenzie, their six-month-old son, Brennan, and two dogs, "Yazzie" and "Bailey." Lisa is a 30-year-old attorney from Ventura, California, of English/German/Hispanic heritage. Pam is a 41-year-old attorney from Chicago, Illinois, of Irish/French-Canadian descent. Since 1992, they have shared a law practice together with a focus on family law. While we did photographs on a Sunday morning, Lisa's mother, Terri — a member of PFLAG, Parents, Families and Friends of Lesbians & Gays — kept her grandkids sitting up and smiling.

Pam: We met playing soccer together in 1991 on a team called the "Hippy Chicks." Then we dated for a year. We had a full-fledged marriage ceremony with relatives flying in from out of state to be part of it. Then we changed our names legally to Liberty-Bibbens, bought a house and got pregnant. We did all the traditional things.

I always knew I wanted to have kids and it was just a matter of getting to a place in life where I felt stable enough and I felt I had the right insurance and enough income to make that commitment. We asked Lisa's younger brother to be a sperm donor and initially he said he wouldn't do it. Then one day out of the blue, he called us up and said that he had reconsidered and volunteered to be our sperm donor. We were tickled pink.

We flew him down to surprise Lisa's mom for Mother's Day. We all went out to brunch and hid him in a big box and he popped out as Lisa's mom's Mother's Day present. I was ovulating at the time. So we had the poor guy in the bathroom with a *Playboy* magazine and a little cup and worked him everyday that he was here. I got pregnant on Mother's Day weekend, which I felt was a good omen. McKenzie was born February 4, 1995.

Lisa: We felt it was as close as we could get to creating a child biologically together. The fact that he was family was important to us. We knew and trusted my brother and knew his health history. We didn't have any concerns that he would later change his mind or give us any legal problems.

Pam: Lisa felt strongly that McKenzie should have a sibling and we talked about her having a child with one of my brothers as the donor. I have a younger brother who I was not close to and didn't spend a lot of time with. I pictured him quite mistakenly as I learned later — as this right-wing Republican and I never thought in a million years he would ever agree. We never thought about asking him and then he volunteered and told my sister if we were still looking for a sperm donor, he would be happy to do it.

We arranged a family vacation where Lisa and McKenzie and I drove to Montana and stayed in a Holiday Inn for a week and then we worked that brother like a workhorse. I remember at the end of our trip, I said, "I bet you're not going to have sex for awhile." And he said, "At least, not by myself." Lisa got pregnant on the very first insemination. She had Brennan just six months ago, in May of this year.

Lisa: We selected names for our children that were not on the Ten Most Popular list. We also wanted names that were unique. Brennan's name was somewhat influenced by William Brennan, the Supreme Court justice.

"I know it sounds like a cliche, but I never realized it would be so wonderful to have little ones be part of our everyday life."

But once we had kids, issues of homophobia began to bother me a lot. I felt like saying, 'All right, everybody! Knock it off right now! I'm not going to put up with this anymore.'

Pam: Lisa has been on a prolonged maternity leave and works two and a half days a week. I work four days a week and Grandma Terri babysits three and a half days a week. We arranged it so that McKenzie and Brennan don't have to be in any kind of day care for their first year. We have a really supportive grandmother.

Lisa: I had no idea how wonderful it would be to parent. I never felt I could love that deeply. I know it sounds like a cliche, but I never realized it would be so wonderful to have little ones be part of our everyday life. What's been the most difficult for me is that I'm a natural worrier and my concerns and worries about the kids have been intensified. I'm concerned about what the world is going to be like when they grow up.

Pam: There's not one thing in my life that I've done that's been more meaningful or more important than having these kids.

My wish is that McKenzie is valedictorian of her class and gets up to make a rousing speech about her two mothers and how wonderful they were throughout her entire childhood. But I too worry about what sort of feedback they're going to get as they get older because they have two moms. I wonder if they're going to want us to go to their sporting events together or what will happen once they hit junior high.

Before we had kids, I did not care that much about homophobia. It didn't affect me in my personal life. I thought if people couldn't understand me being gay, then they had a problem, not me. But once we had kids, issues of homophobia began to bother me a lot. Now it wasn't just affecting me, but it might affect my children. I felt like saying, "All right, everybody! Knock it off right now! I'm not going to put up with this any more."

Lisa: I do think more exposure to lesbian parents with kids will help. There are families that we've been friends with who have never been exposed to lesbian moms. They've learned from us and we've learned from them. Just our family being there with other families and people meeting us as parents helps. They can see we're not whoever they thought we would be and see that our kids are average everyday kids—like theirs.

AMANA JOHNSON WITH HER SONS, KENYETTA AND ALI, DAUGHTER-IN LAW VALORIE, AND GRANDCHILDREN, LAUREN, NAILAH, RASHID, AND MAIYAH

California

Amana Johnson was born in Los Angeles in 1953. She received B.A. degrees in Social Ecology and Comparative Culture from the University of California, Irvine, while raising two sons, Kenyetta (26) and Ali (24) as a single parent. In 1993, she spent six months living in Zimbabwe and South Africa studying the stone carving techniques of Shona and Ndebele sculptors. An internationally known stone sculptor, printmaker and painter, Amana is also a grandmother of four: Nailah (3), Lauren (2), Maiyah (1) and Rashid (9 months). The aroma of baked sweet potatoes wafted through her Oakland home when we arrived on a Sunday afternoon. Amana wore silver bracelets and a mud cloth headdress as she sat among her sons, daughter-in-law Valorie and grandchildren in her backyard.

I feel loved and respected by my sons. I'm very close to both of them and would actually say I feel cherished by them. They're wonderful. They're real allies to me, very supportive of my art and my lifestyle. I think it's a combination of the way they were raised and how close I've always remained to them in bringing them up. I used to go to bat in the women's community because there would be a women's retreat or event and all the boys over six years old couldn't come — even when they were our sons. Well, my sons were a part of me and of the community and they were aware that I was always fighting for them not to be further marginalized.

My grandchildren are just a joy. Maiyah just started walking and Nailah, oh my god, you should see her — she's something else. The four of them spend the night every other weekend. They get out the blow-up pool and Nailah helps me in the garden. Every now and then she tries to whack one of my sculpting stones with a chisel and mallet. All of that is joyous to me. Being a grandmother makes it possible to get the best of both worlds.

It's really important to make sure that my grandchildren and my sons have a respect for diversity and difference. It's important that they understand that there are many choices. That there's not just one barrel of monkeys to jump into. And that our assumptions should not be taken for granted. As a lesbian, I embody one of those differences that counters the social values they're getting at school, from peers and from the media. I'm the one walking off the beaten path.

I had my oldest son, Kenyetta, when I was 16. The boys in my neighborhood where I grew up were very violent and scary to me. I really didn't have much sexual guidance from my mother or any other adults. I came from a single-parent family, so as a child I was really on my own. Consequently I became pregnant early in life.

It was unexpected and traumatic. You could hear the older people talking about "so-and-so's" daughter. I became one of those girls.

I was always interested in learning and school was very important to me. I made sure that I was able to stay in school. I was able to get hooked up with a prenatal-care program for teenage mothers which was very helpful for me — giving me information on how to take care of myself and the children. So I stayed in school, but I was emotionally tormented by the fact that I wasn't married.

> **It's really important to make sure that my grandchildren and my sons have a respect for diversity and difference. It's important that they understand that there are many choices.**

That time was quite stressful. It feels sad, even now — how societal pressures battered my self-esteem. There's a lot of wonderful things that have come from it. Eventually I married Kenyetta and Ali's father when I was about 18. When Kenyetta was nine months old, I moved to North Carolina with his father, who was in the service. I set up a household in a trailer park in Fayetteville. Their father was physically abusive and wouldn't let me go to school. So I saved my money and about six months later, after he went to work, I left with Kenyetta and the t.v.

I came back to Los Angeles and enrolled in L.A. High. I graduated with everyone else in my class but I was still isolated. About a year later I got back together with their father for six months — long enough to conceive Ali. After that, I had a long, unsuccessful period of heterosexuality and homophobia. Eventually I realized I was frantically trying to run from the stereotypes and negative images that I had been fed growing up. I was running from terms like "bulldagger" and "dyke."

When I had my first relationship with a woman, we were in the closet. It wasn't until later that I began to become self-defined and felt like I was making conscious decisions about my sexuality. I began reading literature by Audre Lorde and Barbara Smith and Toni Morrison.

Before the boys began to ask questions, I was already giving them information. I've always been talkative about everything — what I was learning in school, what questions I had as a student. We didn't have a t.v., so we spent our time reading plays, writing songs and talking. In the course of all that, I used our experiences together as a way to interject lessons about life.

It's funny, I remember Ali was more disturbed by my dreadlocks than my sexual preference. I used to have really long dreadlocks, up until a year ago. There are all these negative stereotypes about dreadlocks, and unlike my lesbianism they were blatant and visible.

There are some things that will always be the same in raising children, whether you're gay or straight. As an African-American parent raising young black men to maturity, I have concentrated much of my attention on keeping my sons alive. As black boys and men, they are on the front line in a war for their lives.

I do leadership training with young people who are 16- to 19-year-olds. I have to come out to them. If I don't come out, they will spew out everything that they've ever heard. They'll tell derogatory gay and lesbian jokes. They'll mimic everything they've ever seen or heard. My coming out to them means they have to check themselves. If they do say something, it makes them accountable to me as a human being in the same room. It's important to be open, out, bold and to be intolerant of discrimination.

At the bottom line of it all, there's nothing so particularly magical about being gay or lesbian or bisexual or transgender. Every individual has to work hard to grow into being the best person they can be, regardless of the choices they've made.

For my sons, I wish for them the courage to walk in the darkness of unknown terrain and discover themselves anew throughout their lives. I wish for them the inner vision to dream and live a happy and joyous life.

"At the bottom line of it all, there's nothing so particularly magical about being gay or lesbian or bisexual or transgender."

Leota Lone Dog was born in Manhattan in 1947 and is Lakota, Mohawk and Delaware. She is a Ph.D. student in the American Studies program at N.Y.U., the recipient of a Ford Foundation Predoctoral Fellowship and has been an intern for the American Indian Law Alliance and the Smithsonian Institution. On a warm August afternoon, we sat with her in the kitchen of a West Village apartment she was subletting for the summer. Clustered on the kitchen table were salt and pepper shakers, mixed nuts, a small cactus and various canned goods. A few hours later, her 26-year-old daughter Davida — or "Beanie," as Leota calls her — joined us for pictures on the roof.

There's still a lot of what I do today that has the ramifications of poverty. When I was a kid, we lived in a transient hotel. I had one pair of shoes and one outfit. Looking at myself in the mirror when I was little, the concept of beauty was blonde and I was not that. I was tomboyish. I was constantly trying to get out of the hotel or my uncle's house and build rafts and sail off. When I got my bike, I said, "I have to find these brown people. Where are they?"

I saw us as the "bad guys" because in movies and on t.v., Indians are the bad guys. We rooted for the cowboys. You don't know how to see yourself. Or you see yourself as a stereotype. You romanticize or villainize yourself. You don't see who you really are.

I got pregnant with Beanie when I was 20. I didn't know anything about infants or children. At that point, my mother had disowned me because I had married an African-American. She wanted me to marry Indian and I didn't know any Indian men. At that time, my husband's mother was dying of cancer. She was trying to prepare me for what I needed to know and do. She passed away before Beanie was born. By the time Beanie was born — June of 1969 — I was truly overwhelmed with having this kid with a less-than-ideal husband.

I was realizing that I didn't want to be married and live in the suburbs. On top of it, I thought I was a lesbian. I remember when I was living in the Bronx and I would go to the softball fields and see these really rough dykes. I would look from afar and say, "I don't think so!" Those women looked too hard for me.

I came out in a very ungraceful way. I left home. I left my daughter. It was just awful. I finally decided, after I had left for a weekend, that I needed to go back home and make a decision. I decided to leave and get divorced. I knew I was a lesbian and at that point I didn't need to play the charade.

That was the mid-seventies and somewhere in the *Village Voice* I saw an ad for "Dykes and Tykes," a group in Park Slope, Brooklyn. I went down to see what it was all about. That was the beginning of "You're going to be all right." "Dykes and Tykes" helped me to talk about what I was doing. It also helped Beanie see another side to the husband-and-wife deal — that kids with lesbian mothers are not any less developed or weird or strange because of it.

In 1983, I started seeing and meeting Two-Spirit people at the American Indian Community House. I never saw them in the larger lesbian and gay community, not once. I found that it was much more difficult to be Indian than it was to be a lesbian, for me. I was always on the periphery because no matter how much I was in the lesbian and gay community, I was the only Indian. I wasn't seeing myself. Once I got to the American Indian Community House, I found I was home. Being in my community, being Two-Spirit and being a mother were all working toward a whole of my being.

> " I found that it was much more difficult to be Indian than it was to be a lesbian, for me. I was always on the periphery because no matter how much I was in the lesbian and gay community, I was the only Indian. "

SHERIE LAND AND SARMOD
New Mexico

Sherie Land, age 52, drives a cobalt blue '69 Chevy pick-up and has been a landscaper for the past 12 years. Her 23-year-old son, Sarmod, is half African-American and is visiting her on his way back to Alaska, where he is a full-time fisherman. His African name, "Sarmod," means "freedom of the soul from its earthly bondage." While we talk, Sherie's partner, Katrin, and the couple's two young children play in the room next to us. Although they are a generation apart and live miles apart geographically, Sarmod and his two little sisters are very close and important to each other. After the interview, the two girls jump up and climb on Sarmod as if he were their favorite tree, tossing them from branch to branch in great delight.

We moved to southern California when I was about eight months old. When I was around 13 years old, I met this girl my age at the beach and we became best friends right off. She and I moved into my big, old '41 Chevy sedan together and lived in my car for several months. We were pretty much beach bums except we both had full-time jobs. I would say she was my first true love.

In 1962, I met my future husband in Chicago. I fell madly in love with him. It was true as any love that I had in the past. We lived together for two years and worked in the Civil Rights movement in the sixties. We were married for five years when I got pregnant with Sarmod. Our marriage broke up when I was seven or eight months pregnant and then I moved to San Francisco and had Sarmod there.

I lived with a very good friend. Our relationship was platonic, but we were very close. When we lived in San Francisco, Sarmod was a "latch-key kid." I was working all the time and he would come home and let himself in the house. Every Friday when I got off work, we would take the bus down Haight Street to this fish-and-chips place. The people were great and they loved Sarmod. We always sat at the same table.

This woman who lived on women's land in New Mexico told me all about this land called A.R.F. — 25 acres down in this valley just north of Santa Fe. Sarmod and I moved to Chimayo and met with some of the women who lived there. He was about seven.

My parents ended up coming down on the land with Sarmod and me, and the four of us built a permanent year-round house. We later found that we had all the beams running the wrong way — on the side rather than on the ends. But the house is still standing.

The people who live there are 99 percent lesbians. A.R.F. could stand for "asylum for radical females" or "asylum for rowdy females." No one there at the time really knew.

I never felt discriminated against in New Mexico for being a lesbian. When Sarmod first started school in Chimayo, he definitely was discriminated against — for being half-black in a Hispanic culture. It originated with his teacher, rather than the kids.

When we lived in La Cañada de los Alamos on the other side of the foothills, there was this little shanty village at the end of this road. On the full moon, we would put an air mattress on top of the roof and sleep there. On this one night, there was this incredible meteor shower that we just caught by chance. Sarmod still refers to that all the time.

I want Sarmod to feel good about himself, for who he is and for him to have integrity. I wish that within his lifetime he is witness to a just and understanding world.

> "In 1962, I met my future husband in Chicago. I fell madly in love with him. It was as true as any love that I had in the past."

e drove to the east side of the Cascades, past Sahalie Falls, lava rock and trees turning yellow. On 40 acres of high desert, Joanne Richter and Sara Wiener live with their six-month-old daughter, Bella Michelle, and four llamas, "Mocha," "Curry," "Eddy" and "Wilbur." A Jewish 37-year-old children's clothing designer, Sara was born in New York City to immigrant Russian-Jewish parents. Joanne is a 43-year-old environmental consultant, born in Missoula, Montana, with German, French and Swiss roots. Both avid outdoorswomen and triathletes, Joanne's and Sara's medals and ribbons hang in the baby's room, along with a photograph of Mt. Rainier, the place where they met.

Joanne: I never had any inclination to have children of my own. I don't really like children or relate to children that well — with the exception of those interested in the outdoors. I love to show kids all the neat things there are to explore in nature. When I was a kid, I spent a lot of time outdoors playing with the boys and riding my pony. But I never grew up wanting children. So about six years ago, when Sara would talk about wanting children, I just said, "No way."

Sara: She didn't say, "No way." She would say, "I think I can support you having a child, but I will not be a co-parent." We pursued our relationship knowing Joanne was not very interested in kids.

Joanne: Finally, it became such a strong urge for Sara, that we were either going to break up because I didn't want a family or because I'd imposed my feelings on her and prevented her from having a child.

Sara: One day, I was crying hysterically and said, "I'm having a child." That was it. It came to that cathartic moment of truth.

Joanne: I realized we'd take it day by day, and it was really a miracle for me to see Sara pregnant.

Sara: We wanted Bella to know her donor. We didn't want there to be any secrets or hidden information. And it was clear we wanted a donor and not a father. I had been looking at a friend of ours for awhile and saying what a great guy he was. Joanne thought he was a good choice. He's straight and had been single for some time. One day I said to him, "I have a really big question to ask you and you don't have to answer me right now. But just think about it." After I asked him, he said, "Uh hum. That is a big question." We continued to talk about it over meals and process the many questions and issues.

Eventually he agreed. I knew when I was fertile, so I inseminated four days in a row. I did get pregnant that first month.

Joanne: While Sara was pregnant, I was still processing my feelings and gradually getting used to the idea. Even though I was her labor and delivery coach, I didn't really know how I was going to participate.

Sara: The real transformation was when Bella was born.

Joanne: It was a turning point watching this little being come out of Sara. The most amazing thing for me was when Bella's head came out. She was purple and not breathing because she was still attached

> **One day, I was crying hysterically and said, 'I'm having a child.' That was it. It came to that cathartic moment of truth.**

and hid in France. My mother and aunt were hidden in a convent where the nuns took the Jewish kids in. My grandmother was a very brave woman and survived the war. She lost her parents, her aunts, uncles, eight siblings — everybody except two brothers, and she still had an unsinkable spirit. She was my best friend. She was the strongest figure in my life and the best role model and female figure. It wasn't even a question that my little girl would be named after her.

Joanne: As Bella's parent, I want to instill in her really good values so that she can cope in this world that scares the hell out of me. One of the reasons I was so against having kids initially is, I really feel this world has way too many people in it already. I have an incredible life with a lot of opportunities and I'm not sure Bella is going to have those same opportunities — particularly to be out in nature and open space in a relatively unpolluted world. This kid's going to have to deal with tremendous difficulties worldwide and environmental challenges. Personally, I didn't feel like I could bring a child into that kind of environment. Now that we have, I feel we have to prepare her as best we can.

inside. She almost looked like some creature from outer space, and then a moment later, the full Bella came slipping out. Just holding her and feeling that warmth and life was amazing.

Sara: When we found out we were having a girl, there wasn't even a question what her name was going to be. I didn't need to look in any name books. Her name, "Bella Michelle" comes from my maternal grandmother, who was an incredibly strong woman. She was born in Russia in the Ukraine. As a young girl, she went to Germany to study logic and she married my grandfather. They fled Hamburg the last day of '38

Miriam Messinger lives with her partner, Felicia Hayes, in a three-story house in Roxbury. They have an upright piano in the foyer and lots of painted masks and a soapstone menora on the dining room mantel. Born and raised in New York City, and the daughter of noted political figure, Ruth Messinger, Miriam is a public health educator of Jewish/Polish/Russian ancestry. Felicia is an African-American high school humanities teacher who was raised upstate. They have been together for 10 years and have a two-year-old daughter, Amani, who sat in her high chair eating strawberries wearing her Minnie Mouse bib. A very private person, Felicia declined to be interviewed.

I grew up in a very progressive setting. When I was three, my parents bought a brownstone on the Upper West Side of Manhattan. They couldn't really afford it, so they ended up forming a collective household. People rented rooms and everyone shared in making dinner. It ended up being a community. Both my parents were politically involved in the Civil Rights movement, the peace movement and the women's movement. I grew up knowing that it's our responsibility in the world to confront injustice. So there were always meetings at my house. Some of the people who lived with us were gay or lesbian. It was clear that it was accepted.

In 1988, I had just finished writing my thesis at Harvard when I met Felicia. I had just come out and had just broken up with my first lover. I went with some friends to a lesbian bar. They asked me if I had ever asked a woman to dance. I said, "No" and looked around and decided who I liked dancing and it was Felicia. I asked her to dance and we ended up dancing together a long time that night. We started dating shortly after that. I made her dinner one night and we've been together ever since.

I think we might have had a child sooner, but because we're an interracial lesbian couple, issues of racism, homophobia, class and religious differences are part of our daily lives. As conscious parents, we were examining what we needed to give our child in order for her to be strong and capable. Also, how to create a community that fully supports who we are as a family, and how to slowly change the rest of the world so that it is a safer place to be.

We had a lot of discussions, but eventually we were ready to take the leap. Once I was pregnant, we decided whatever issue came up, we'd deal with it. We chose an anonymous, African-American donor through a sperm bank. I got pregnant on our first insemination at our doctor's office. Felicia was reading poetry and stroking my stomach. We had candles and incense burning. I had a great pregnancy. We read to the baby and sang to her. We posted the amniocentesis pictures on our kitchen wall. My mom gave us a big baby shower in New York and we got endless hand-me-downs from my brother's child.

We had a naming ceremony for Amani when she was three months old to welcome her into a larger community. We tried to respect a variety of cultures and traditions she comes from. We used some things from Yoruba and other African traditions and some traditional Jewish prayers. We wanted to honor the meaning of her name. "Amani" is Swahili for "peace." And her middle name is "Ariel," which is Hebrew for "Lioness of God." Her name feels fierce and beautiful to me.

I really wanted to be able to offer Felicia and Amani a warm and loving extended family. On some levels, there's been a lot of disappointment. If Felicia and Amani and I go to a family event and there are 150 people at the wedding and Felicia and Amani are the only African-Americans there, my family doesn't see that as an incredibly uncomfortable place for us to be. On some level, it's sending a message to Amani that the people we value most and care about the most and manage to have in our circle are all white. Coming from a family that sees itself as liberal or progressive, it is sometimes even harder to confront issues of personal responsibility. It is our hope that in the future we will improve these extended family relationships — for ourselves and for Amani.

KAREN MORRISON, AUDREY MORRISON AND KINSEY
Arizona

*J*hirteen-month-old Kinsey Morrison lives with her moms, Karen and Audrey, and her 85-year-old great-grandmother. "Maybe it's just me," said Granny, "but of my 23 great-grandchildren, she's the smartest and the prettiest baby we've ever had in this family. It's the truth." Although now a 35-year-old chief operating officer for the American Red Cross, Karen met Audrey 18 years ago when Audrey was her high school English teacher in Louisville, Kentucky. Both lovers of literature, they named Kinsey after Kentucky mystery writer Sue Grafton's main character — Kinsey Millhone — who has a "tough and independent spirit and thinks for herself."

> **"** ... I always remind her that Ward and June Cleaver would have been an embarrassment to Beaver eventually. **"**

Karen: What's funny is that when people find out that Audrey was my high school teacher, they assume she seduced me. I was 17 when I met her and she was 31, but it took me 13 years to get her to realize I was something more than a pesky kid, bright and a little endearing and sometimes interesting to talk to.

I was 30 years old by then. I always wanted a stable, secure home environment and a committed relationship where children knew they were safe and loved. Both Audrey and I grew up in homes where things could fall apart at any minute and did frequently. We both had a strong drive to create something different and do it better.

Audrey: When Karen says she is afraid that Kinsey will grow up to be embarrassed about her parents, I always remind her that Ward and June Cleaver would have been an embarrassment to Beaver eventually.

Karen: We selected an anonymous donor. After several months of inseminating, I was diagnosed with endometriosis. I switched doctors and had a GIFT procedure — a Gamete Intra-Fallopian Transer. My first question when I woke up was, "Did it work?"

Audrey: Two weeks later, Karen sent me 13 red roses with a message she was pregnant.

Karen: A friend of mine once said that his feeling about children was, "Being born was enough. Anything else they do is gravy." Just their birth ought to make you happy.

Audrey: I remember the day Karen came home from work and I was excited to show her that Kinsey could stand by herself. As Karen sat in front of the couch, I said, "Sweetheart, look at this!" and turned her loose to stand by herself and Kinsey walked a couple steps toward her. Now, she's walking all over the place.

Karen: My greatest joy is just watching her grow and laugh and learn. One night, after her bath, she was really laughing at being tickled and I thought, "That sound is worth everything we went through to get her."

Massachusetts

"One thing I always shared with my children is that I am a mother and I am also a human being. I am multi-dimensional. As much as I have responsibility towards them, I am also responsible for myself."

In late September, we rode the Amtrak to Boston, passing stone walls, white clapboard houses, sailboats, industrial eyesores and a few scarlet and gold trees. We took a cab to Antonieta Gimeno Cardona's house in a working-class neighborhood in Jamaica Plain where her 18-year-old daughters, Lucia and Yuisa and cat "Cubitos" were hanging out on the front porch. Born in Panama City in 1942, Antonieta was raised in Mexico City and is a mixed Mexican-El Salvadorian. Although currently Program Director for the Boston Women's Fund, Antonieta said with a wink, "Some day, I'll move west, ride a motorcycle and smoke cigars." While we were there, teenagers of all colors and sexual identities found refuge in Antonieta's kitchen, where Spanish and English merged into one sound.

When I became pregnant, I was 36 years old. I met Lucia and Yuisa's father through friends of mine. He's Puerto Rican and black and was living in the Bronx. I decided he was going to be the father, but I didn't want to have a relationship with him. I told him I wanted children. There was a rhythm in my body, my soul and my spirit that said this was the time, that everything was ready for me. When the ultrasound showed I was going to have twins, I cried and laughed at the same time. It was a very powerful feeling that I had inside of me. I had the most perfect pregnancy I could ever dream of. I was centered and in total harmony with myself and everybody else.

One thing I always shared with my children is that I am a mother, and I am also a human being. I am multi-dimensional. As much as I have responsibility toward them, I also am responsible for myself. In Mexican culture, mothers are the virgins and the saints. You give and sacrifice all and have not a minute of pleasure for yourself. Being a good mother in my culture means you don't have a sexuality.

That's a big burden the world has placed on mothers: to be all for everybody, to be the nurturer, the cook, the washerwoman, pick the kids up, do homework together and take care of everybody. And to say, "I don't need anything. I don't deserve anything for myself." I don't buy that. There are times when I didn't want to be a mother. I remember at one point I felt suicidal and that I couldn't handle it. It's hard to be so honest because I'm afraid I'll get judged as not being a "good mother." There's a lot of investment from society in putting women in the role of "perfect mother" and provider. It's like a chain to keep you in place. Because if you're not a mother, what else can you be? Can you have dreams?

When Lucia and Yuisa were in the first grade, their teachers felt they were not going to do very well in school. They were asked to repeat the first grade. I became angry and asked for an explanation and an evaluation. So they did one. Evaluations are a funny thing — I don't have a lot of trust in the system, but I wanted to make sure Lucia and Yuisa were okay. The tests showed there was some kind of difficulty with spatial relationships, so they recommended a speech therapist. I didn't know what the hell speech therapy had to do with spatial relations, but I said okay. They again told me my children would not go very far in academics.

How I dealt with it is I immersed myself with them and made sure they got everything they needed. I was always there with them to do homework. As a result, my kids are very intelligent and articulate. I don't think they have any problems. It was scary — if you really believe what psychologists say, you can destroy a child's life. Lucia and Yuisa and I were diagnosed as a "fail-ure-to-thrive" family because when they were little, they were really tiny and the doctors were afraid that I wasn't doing a good job. As soon as the doctors look at you through a certain lens and put a stamp on you, it's very hard to get rid of — you're a "failure-to-thrive" until the day you die. I told them there was no problem and my children were growing and developing and walking and talking just fine.

I am a very stubborn woman. To me, obstacles are probably the thing that make me want to go further. I have worked very hard and I think Lucia and Yuisa can do anything they want. They have surpassed their teachers. Besides putting a roof over their heads, I have guided them, listened to them and valued them. I trust and believe in them. I feel strongly about things and I have never shied away from telling my kids how I see the world, politically and spiritually. We have always had dialogues and my kids are incredibly articulate. We discuss what racism and classism are about. I said to Lucia and Yuisa, "When you are sure about something within yourself, then the rest will follow. If you're conveying fear or doubt, then they will eat you alive."

Because of the color of my skin, I don't fit into this black and white dialogue in this country. That has pre-sented a lot of painful and difficult situations for us. I used to think that identity was something you were born with. I didn't realize identity was something that you forged, that you work with and that changes with the pas-sage of time. As I have come to terms with the racial mix that I have in myself, now I can say, "I am a mestiza."

Working to be "out" is a daily thing. It's about taking a stand and being proud of being a mestiza, a Mexicana-Salvadorian, and of being working class and the values that come with that. And being ready to say, "Yes, I am a lesbian." Then you'll know who your true friends are.

"It's about taking a stand and being proud of being a mestiza, a Mexicana-Salvadorian, and of being working class and the values that come with that. And being ready to say, 'Yes, I am a lesbian.'"

Catherine Carhart and Ann Hollingsworth live in an old and historic town in rural New Mexico. We drove past chamisa, tall cottonwoods and burnt umber salt cedar. Deep-cut arroyos and contours of earth led us to their house. Born in San Mateo, California, in 1957, Catherine is a software designer and businesswoman. Ann, a builder and artist, was born in Washington, D.C., in 1953. Their three-year-old son, Gabriel, conceived through anonymous donor insemination, was coloring at the kitchen table when we arrived. His buckskin jacket and a big dream catcher hung behind him on the wall. Ann and Catherine were sipping coffee beside him. Later they saddled Santana, their palamino, for the family portrait.

Catherine: Ann and I met when she remodeled my house in California in 1988. I had just sold my software company and was ripe to change my life completely. I knew that I wanted to have children before I met her, but I didn't want to be an absentee parent, in a position of working so hard that my partner and I weren't together enough to be a family. After I got together with Ann, and was able to carve out time and space for a family, I wanted to create more members to our family right away.

Ann: I kept saying, "Why don't we be romantic for another year?"

Catherine: So we waited. It took a few years, as it turned out, for us to free up our time at our businesses and then to conceive.

Ann: Also, I thought we ought to know each other longer.

Catherine: Having a really stable relationship was very important, and that has been really good. Particularly since Ann was able to adopt Gabe, we are both the legal parents of this child.

Ann: When Gabe was one, I adopted him. In California, second parent adoptions are being approved routinely in some counties, but are not possible in others. Here in New Mexico, we understand that they are quietly approved. I didn't think that psychologically it would make any difference in terms of the depth of my commitment, but it did — to him, me and Catherine. Catherine was more the primary parent the first year because of breastfeeding. She seemed to have more claim to him because she had given birth to him. I felt more like the "nice aunt" or the "second-loving-person." When I adopted him, I made a commitment to take care of him for the rest of my life, legally. There was a depth to that. It felt very profound to me.

It also felt very ironic that Catherine and I can't be married, but I could adopt Gabriel. I made this incredible commitment to our family, but I can't make it to my partner. I've never been into gay marriage or commitment ceremonies. They never held much meaning for me. But now I'm very attached to the intention of that legal contract.

Catherine: As a family, I feel we are protected by the resources we have in terms of community, money in the bank and stable families around us that will give us support. I think that level of security makes it pretty easy to pass on a sense of security to Gabriel. We know that there are people who will never approve of our family. We want to protect Gabe from hatred until he has the inner strength and wisdom to understand and protect himself.

" As a family, I feel we are protected by the resources we have in terms of community, money in the bank and stable families around us that will give us support. **"**

I think by choosing where you live and how you live, we can give Gabe a much easier life for a much longer time. That's one of the reasons why living in our other home in Berkeley for part of the year is so important to me. There are so many lesbian families that it's as close to "normal" as any other family.

The fact that we're lesbians and we really wanted him and we worked really hard to bring him into our family makes it all the more likely that we're going to make a lot of room for him in our lives. I think that has been good for him.

Ann: When I realized that I was gay, in the mid-seventies, I assumed that I would never be a parent. Now, getting to be a parent feels like a tremendous gift.

Emotionally I feel very open and the things that have been the most difficult for me are all the things in my own life that I carry around — things that were said or done to me as a child that I definitely see again as an adult in the context of my child growing up.

Catherine: Trying to parent differently than your parents raised you can leave you on shaky ground. You have to find a new way between you and your child. For example, I was raised to not talk about emotions. With Gabriel, we're raising him in a much more open way: "Why are you upset?" "How did that feel?" His emotional language is probably greater at this age than mine is now!

Also, to make sure that you don't convey shame to the child, you really have to root out your own shame and homophobia so that he is comfortable having lesbian parents. But the greatest challenges we've faced have been the challenges of parenthood common to all couples, such as getting him to eat, to sleep, figuring out how to introduce sexuality. How do you explain death? How do you explain war? How do you teach him that you can't take a stick and hit another child, or how do you explain when he just got hit by another kid?

Postscript: *Since this interview, Ann and Catherine had a second child, Samuel. He was born at home in August of 1997. Gabriel is delighted to have a brother.*

Sam, Risa and Gabriella were sitting on their front driveway eating baloney and cheese sandwiches with black olives on a Tuesday afternoon. They are the three-year-old triplets of Mimi Luther, a 39-year-old health care professional, and her ex-partner, Sheila, with whom she shares custody. After lunch, the triplets put on their sunglasses, got on their bikes and headed down the street. Later that afternoon, Mimi laid them down for a nap in a room with three little beds, a painted rainbow on the ceiling and a big rabbit on the wall. Talkative, affectionate and energetic, the triplets told us that they were all going to trampoline class after their naps.

I've known forever that I'm "mommy" material. When I got together with Sheila, one of the things I told her in the very beginning was, "I'm going to be a mom." About five years into our relationship, we started pursuing it. We chose an anonymous donor from a sperm bank who was Mexican and married with three kids of his own. I ordered the sperm with my Visa by phone. They shipped it here on a U.P.S. truck. Every time I see a U.P.S. truck now, I just smile because you never know what's on those trucks.

When I went in for a pregnancy test and had an ultrasound, I saw three little black spheres. In walks the doctor and I said, "There's three!" He said, "Oh my god, I better sit down."

By the fifth month, I looked like I was nine months pregnant. I was put on bed rest at seven months with home uterine monitoring. I wasn't supposed to be out of bed at all. When I would get out of bed, I would have up to 17 contractions every hour. It was hard. I was so big I got stuck in the bathtub. I had 15 pounds of baby in me.

During the whole pregnancy, Sam had his head down in my pelvic area and when he would turn his head, I could feel it in my pelvic bone. Risa was always over on the right side and was a little acrobat. She used to flip flop all the time and do somersaults. Gabby was my surprise baby. She was always much smaller than the other two. She was way up under my ribs. On the ultrasound, she looked like a fossil of a vertebrate animal, like a little curled up snail or figurine. She didn't move around much.

I had the kids the day before my 36th birthday. They were born C-section on May 17, 1994. Sam was 5 lbs. 1 oz. Risa was 4 lbs. 14 oz. And Gabby was 3 lbs. 11 oz. In the delivery room, they had a doctor, a nurse, an anesthesiologist and respiratory therapist for each baby.

When they were two and a half months old, we had a wonderful ceremony appointing "soul-watchers" for each child, our version of godparents. We chose four adults for each child who agreed to serve that traditional godparent role and give the kids things that we couldn't give to them — whether that was spiritual, emotional or physical — and keep sight over them forever, throughout their entire lives. I knew that there would be stuff that they would need that Sheila or I couldn't give them. It might be something as simple as practicing basketball. That's not in my make-up. Or it might be something as complex as a discussion about sexuality that they wouldn't feel comfortable approaching me about.

The moments that I cherish the most with them happen without any planning, when I catch sight of them and realize that they're my children. I'm so busy all the time. If I'm not at work, I'm going to make dinner or doing four more loads of laundry or the cats are hungry or Risa and Sam are fighting. I feel like what my mom used to call "chief cook and bottle-washer." When they are outside playing and I am in the kitchen doing the dishes, I look out the window and see Risa pushing Sam and Gabby on the little glider — times like that touch a part of me where I forget everything else for the moment and the rest of the world washes away.

My greatest challenge has been this split with Sheila. I never imagined it would ever happen — even in my wildest dreams. I'm so disappointed that my kids are going to be the children of a divorce. I just hate that. I know we can manage to find our way together, but it's hard on a daily basis. Trying to explain to the kids what's happened to their family now is really hard.

I would tell anybody considering parenthood that when you do have kids, it's important to get away from them sometimes and keep some piece of your relationship with your partner sacred. Even if it means that you have to write in your datebook that you're going for a walk every Saturday morning. Even if you don't feel like doing it, do it anyway. Don't give up your space alone and that kind of sacred privacy.

My assistant at my job, Kellie, is a devout Christian. She's married with two kids and lives in the suburbs. And I'm a really "out" lesbian mom. Over the last two years, we have become such good, close friends. On the surface, we have nothing in common. Our politics are different. Our faith is different. Our values are different. But through our kids, we have more in common than anybody could have ever guessed. She's been there for me in a way not many people have. In many ways, we are not that different from each other. We are just moms.

" ... times like that touch a part of me where I forget everything else for the moment and the rest of the world washes away. "

BEVERLY LITTLE THUNDER AND LUSHANYA
Arizona

Beverly Little Thunder lives close to the Mexican border with two canaries and a cockatoo. She is a nurse specializing in case management for **HIV** and **AIDS** in Cochise County. A 49-year-old mother and grandmother, Beverly is a Sundance Pipecarrier of the Lakota Nation who now leads the Wimmin's Sundance. In 1985, she was asked to leave her own people for being lesbian. Inside her double-wide mobile home is a dried century plant covered with red chile lights, a squash blossom maiden print and *Out* magazine on the coffee table. A storyteller who laughs easily, she is photographed here with her youngest daughter, Lushanya.

In the Lakota tradition, there's a story about when someone who was born having the spirit of both male and female, being able to understand the male and female components. So they were born Two-Spirit. From that, it's become a contemporary term that a lot of lesbian and gay men in the Native community have adopted as a marker for who they are. However, the term Two-Spirit does not translate into any native tongue.

In our tribe, lesbians were called *koskalakawin.* Historically, they were the women who were trained to take care of the other women who had female problems. They usually opted not to marry. They were the women who adopted orphaned children. They became the aunties and the grandmothers to all the children of the tribe. They held prominent positions in ceremony.

In retrospect, the first time I think I realized that I was attracted to women, I must have been eight years old. I remember walking outside the Greyhound bus station in L.A. There was this woman standing against the wall, smoking a cigarette. She had the most beautiful green eyes I've ever seen. Her hair was slicked back in a duck-tail and she was wearing men's attire and men's shoes. I looked up at her and she smiled.

I am a traditionalist and have raised my family in the ways of the Lakota people. I am a Two-Spirit mother of five. I have three children who live in Arizona and one who lives in northern California and a son in Washington. I have two granddaughters and one grandson. One of my daughters is a firefighter and the other, Lushanya, is an "out" lesbian going to school full-time. Lushanya means "hummingbird" in Arapaho.

One of my sons seems to love being in jail and another is an arrogant male most of the time. All three of my sons do have a gentle side that they try to hide at times.

I got married when I was 15, to get out of the house because of my mother's alcoholism. I spent a lot of my childhood with my grandmother in South Dakota. When I got pregnant, I thought, well, I can't be lesbian because I'm pregnant. I thought I must be normal because I viewed being lesbian as abnormal.

I came out to my children when my youngest was eight years old. I got the kids together and we sat down and had a "talking circle." We passed an eagle feather. My two oldest boys said, "Well, whatever you want, as long as you're happy." My oldest daughter was mortified. She had a really hard time with it.

My greatest challenge as a mother is allowing my children to be who they need to be, regardless of what path they're on. It's real painful sometimes to allow them to do what they need to do.

I don't think homophobia is something that can be fought. It's important that each of us really believes that we have the right to truly be who we are and that we have a right to be here. It doesn't matter what anybody else thinks. We need to just go about our lives.

> **In the Lakota tradition, there's a story about when someone who was born having the spirit of both male and female, being able to understand the male and female components. So they were born Two-Spirit.**

SUE THEISSEN AND JAE DOUGLAS WITH JAMIE, JOE AND LUCY
Oregon

Sue Theissen and Jae Douglas live in a four-bedroom colonial in Mount Tabor with their five-year-old daughter Lucy, two cats, "L.C." and "Noah," and "Libby" the dog. Jae is a 37-year-old administrator and social worker who grew up in Providence, Rhode Island, and is "mostly Irish." Sue is a 43-year-old entrepreneur from Twin Falls, Idaho, who is Norwegian, English and Welsh. Born and raised as a devout Mormon, Sue married her high school English teacher and has two grown children, Jamie (24) and Joe (22). On a rainy weekday afternoon, they all patiently gathered on the backyard deck surrounded by western hemlocks. When it stopped raining for 15 minutes, everyone fell easily into place for photographs.

Jae: We've been together nine years and married for eight years. When we had been together for six months, we started talking about commitment. We were sitting at *Machismo Mouse,* a fast food Mexican restaurant in Clackamas County, which is pretty conservative. Sue said, "So do you want to get married?" I screamed and ran into the bathroom and made quite a scene. I came back out and said, "Yes!"

We got married in an old non-denominational church with lots of stained glass and candles. We had a hundred or so people at the wedding — all the important people in our lives. The kids sang for us. We exchanged vows and rings. Sue got me a bagpiper. For me, being Celtic, it made it much more magical.

Sue: My pants and jacket were made of raw silk. We wore kimonos and I had a bright green shell underneath. Jae wore a purple one. She wore heels and I had regular green suede shoes. We found a jeweler to make our rings. We had cake and played music and people danced. It was a wonderful evening.

When Jae and I got together, she welcomed my children with open arms and considered them her children and acted as a parent. She and Jamie and Joe formed a very special and important relationship quickly. That's the beginning of how our family came together.

Jae: Lucy was conceived at home in 1991. I had known her father since 1986. We had been talking a long time about it. I come from a long line of fertile women, so it only took two inseminations. At her birth, her father was there and his lover, Rick. Joe was there and two other good friends. She was born January 6, 1992.

Sue: Jae and I parent easily together. My theory on how to raise happy, healthy children who can contribute to the world in a positive way is simply loving them. Lots of love, acceptance and reinforcement for all the good stuff. Being kind, considerate and truthful were values I carry on from my parents and I hope have passed on to my kids. And letting them know they're perfect just the way they are. I can pass on my values to them and trust that at some point, they get to make their own decisions. Their decisions might not match mine and that's got to be okay.

Jae: Until you have children, there's a certain freedom to be selfish and indulge your own ego. When you have kids, that stops. There are days when I am paying attention to what Jamie needs and what Joe needs and Lucy needs and I put my own needs aside. That takes a lot of energy. In the process, I'm also seeing who they really are and who they're becoming in the world and supporting that process.

> "Sue said, 'So do you want to get married?' I screamed and ran into the bathroom and made quite a scene. I came back out and said, 'Yes!'"

Whether it's dealing with the fact that they're trying to learn to read or negotiating a romantic relationship or dealing with their own fears or confidence, as a parent, I have to be attentive to all of that. Sometimes it comes easily and I feel very gracious and magnanimous. Other times, you hope nobody is watching.

Sue: In our family, the simple moments are what's meaningful, when there's a connection. Jae and I watch the children together and they each have different gifts and talents. Joe is a singer. I remember the first time I heard him sing an opera. Everything welled up inside of me and it wasn't anything but his own gift. It had nothing to do with me. It touched my heart.

Jae: Sometimes Jamie will bring a crowd of 20-somethings into the house with all their 20-something energy. Other times, it will be Lucy and all her five-year-old friends and all that kid energy. Whether it's a small kid or the big kids, the house comes alive. It sort of crackles. Those are the times I stop and vividly remember to breathe it in and feel how great it is to have a big, noisy, happy house.

The rich moments are also at the end of the day when Sue and I will lay in bed together and we'll talk about the kids one by one.

Sometimes, we've found that the kids are the only thing we have to talk about and when that happens, I say, "Oh, I think we better go see a movie or maybe we ought to read a book together." We try to keep our relationship with each other and our relationship with the children in balance. But there's nothing like watching someone you love, love your children. When you know that it's coming from the inside out, it's an amazing thing.

Black and white photographs from Brazil cover the walls of Linda Villarosa and Vickie Starr's living room. They are the work of Lorry Salcedo, a gay photographer from Peru, who is also the father of Linda and Vickie's baby daughter, Kali. With terracotta-colored skin, black hair, indigo eyes, Kali was just three weeks old when we arrived at their brownstone in New York. A well-known couple in the New York dyke community, Linda is the former executive editor at *Essence* magazine and Vickie is a music publicist and former music editor for *Outweek*. During their interview, Kali was nursing, an orange cat named "Scruffy" wandered around, and Vickie picked cherry tomatoes from their backyard garden for everyone.

Linda: Vickie and I first met in 1991. She was working at *Outweek* magazine, and they were going to do a story on me. Then I ran into her again at Gay Pride.

Vickie: The first time I met Linda, I thought she was cute, but she totally dissed me. I asked her out on a date and she brought six of her friends.

Linda: I was just testing the waters, to see how she responded under stress. (Laughs) As for having kids, I had wanted to have a baby for a long time and it never quite worked out with anyone until I got together with Vickie. She definitely wanted kids, although she didn't want to have a baby as soon as I wanted to. I was very serious because I felt like I was getting older — I'm 37.

Vickie: Linda was on a different schedule than I was, and she just kept bugging me until I broke down.

Linda: We had to make some compromises. We went to therapy and we talked about it constantly.

Vickie: At one point, it actually did come down to Linda doing this with me or on her own. I couldn't imagine us being girlfriends and her having a child without it also being my child. That just didn't make any sense.

Linda: I always knew I wanted to have kids mainly because my mother and the women in my family talked about mothering in such a positive way. It was never like you won't do it because you're a lesbian.

Vickie: In terms of choosing a sperm donor, the first question was race. Linda wanted a black sperm donor partly because her family lineage is so mixed that she was afraid if she had a baby with a white man, the baby would look white and grow up to be treated as white and that part of her heritage would disappear. So we went on this

> "Linda wanted a black sperm donor partly because her family lineage is so mixed that she was afraid if she had a baby with a white man, the baby would look white and grow up to be treated as white and that part of her heritage would disappear."

search for a black man. We felt like we wanted to know the sperm donor and wanted preferably a gay man. It took us a year to negotiate all the social issues of how the family would be structured with this one guy, only to find out in the end that he was not fertile.

Linda: Then we decided on a sperm bank in California. But it was expensive, invasive, inconvenient and clinical. We tried it for a few months, but it wasn't going well.

Vickie: Linda was getting more depressed every month because she wasn't getting pregnant and we were spending all this money.

Linda: Finally, in October, on the day that the O. J. Simpson criminal verdict came down, I came to Vickie and said, "Let's go with Lorry." Lorry has been a close friend of Vickie's for ten years; he wanted to be a parent and they had discussed having a child together. But we had originally decided not to use him because he wasn't black. Then after all the difficulties we were having trying to get pregnant, I started to feel like race was interfering with and complicating my ability to make a decision about the sperm donor.

Vickie: It's significant that it was the day of the O.J. verdict. All these black women Linda works with were depressed because people were so confused and disgusted about the complexity of the O.J. case. Linda looked at me and said, "Call Lorry." We called Lorry and it turns out he had just been waiting for us to change our minds about using him. A couple days before Thanksgiving, Lorry came over and Linda got pregnant on the first try.

Linda: When I found out I was pregnant, I was really happy because it had been such a long process ... Kali was born at 36 weeks on July 15 at Mount Sinai in Manhattan. My doctor is a lesbian mother, so we got great treatment in the hospital. A resident came in and I had never seen him before and Vickie was in the single bed with me. He said, "Oh, I need to take your temperature. Which one of you had the baby?"

Vickie: Now that we have a kid, I think it's interesting what a leveler being a parent is. Where before we may have felt more conscious of being gay in our day-to-day lives, now we have conversations with strangers on the street who happen to be holding a four-month-old baby. On an emotional level, you have a child and you feel love for the child. Sexual orientation seems to have very little to do with it.

Linda: In terms of our family dynamic we're trying to create a relationship with three parents.

Vickie: I feel we're very privileged: Kali has three parents who love her and who are emotionally and materially equipped to take very good care of her.

Linda: I just hope she knows she's loved and that she's cared for. I hope she understands what we went through to get her and that she has a whole community of people supporting her including us and our families.

> **On an emotional level, you have a child and you feel love for the child. Sexual orientation seems to have very little to do with it.**

PAM LOUIE AND ROBERT
California

Pam Louie is a 33-year-old divisional controller for a company in Napa Valley. She lives in a light pink house with skylights, wood floors and a breathtaking view of San Francisco from the back deck. When we arrived on a Saturday morning, she was wearing a Rutgers sweatshirt and studying for her C.P.A exam. Her 16-year-old son, Robert, was eating a bowl of "Crunch Berries," sitting quietly at the dining room table. Her two nephews were watching t.v. downstairs and playing with the dog "Cleo" and cat "Tigger."

I was born in Oakland/Chinatown in 1962. My mom is Hawai'ian, Mexican, Filipino and American Indian and my dad is Chinese. I was born into a working class family. My mother was a migrant farm worker during her childhood and later became a beautician. My dad's family came from China around 1920 and spoke very little English. He died when he was 45. With six other sisters and 16 nieces and nephews, we're bursting out of the seams in our family. Recently there was a family reunion in Hawai'i where over 2,500 people attended and that wasn't even the whole family.

I was pregnant when I was 15 and had Robert when I was 16. He was born on the 22nd of March, 1979. His father is part Portuguese and white and denied his paternity. I have not talked to his father since Robert was born.

I took care of Robert for three years. During that time, I was experimenting with women and I defined myself as a lesbian, but I had a child to think about. I was working nights — midnight to 7 a.m. — as a warehouse clerk. I had dropped out of school, but wanted to go on to college. For those first three years, I was really confused. My sister and her husband were very concerned and they decided to legally adopt him. In retrospect, I wish I had the courage and strength to take on the role of mother at that age, but I wasn't ready. I know I could not have given him the quality and time that he needed. He went with my sister and they did a wonderful job.

Eventually my sister told him I was his biological mom. Just recently he's come to live with me and we're still in this process of learning about each other. He doesn't call me "Mom." It feels awkward, even though maternally I am. He usually calls me "Pam." He basically has two moms. I feel indebted to my sister for taking care of him and bringing him up to be such a warm and caring person. Robert's a great gift. After all that he's been through, he has a strong soul and a loving heart.

Education is important to me, and being able to open yourself to knowledge. I would like Robert to expand his literary reading to include the classics. In order for Robert to go to Hawai'i this year with me, I said, "You have to read *Moby Dick* and *The Scarlet Letter.*" He's also at an age of being sexually curious. I told him, "I can't tell you not to have sex, but you need to be smart about it. HIV is on the rise with teenagers. You need to be safe because I don't want anything happening to you."

I know he needs my guidance. I want to instill in Robert the value of human life, that it's important to value all people, cultures and religions. When you develop that from within, it will travel from one generation to the next. Once he said something about "those Chinese people" and I said, "Excuse me. You're part Chinese yourself." It's hard being multi-ethnic and coming to terms with who you are. Nothing makes you better than the person next to you. I want him to understand the differences and the commonalities within all people in the human race.

> "I was pregnant when I was 15 and had Robert when I was 16. I have not talked to his father since Robert was born."

With her swaying, long, brown hair, Karen Schoonmaker looks like a teenager at first glance. But for more than a decade she has supported her three children, working as a baker, a videographer and currently as a real estate broker in the hotel industry. Josh, Miriam and Zach (ages ten, eight and six) were outside eating burritos when we arrived and they quickly gathered around us, curious about our questions and eager to contribute their opinions on homophobia and racism. They offered an array of insights — articulate, humorous and poignant. Six-year-old Zach finally stated, "If everyone in the world was the same, it would be so dull." Then they all ran off and jumped on their bikes, a blur of baggy pants and blinking high-tops.

I was born in California in 1963 and grew up in Texas, near Houston. I am of European descent — French, German and Dutch — and I was basically raised Catholic. My mother was a devout Catholic until my parents divorced when I was 10.

I left home when I was 17 and went to college for a year and then moved to New York. I was pregnant three months later. My children have two different fathers. I married the second man with whom I had two of the children. We were together for a year and a half, long enough for me to get pregnant twice. I waited almost four years after we separated before I filed for divorce, enough time to get stronger and get my life together. I felt like I understood exactly how I wanted to negotiate through the system and get what I wanted. I certainly knew women who had fear about their children being taken away from them and I didn't want to have to worry about that.

During that time I slept with men and women. I don't know how other people would classify my life. I've never thought of myself as bisexual. I would have year-long stretches when I slept only with women or year-long stretches when I slept only with men. But I never mixed the two. I certainly am lesbian-identified now and have been for six years.

In New Mexico, I went into the divorce process with a lawyer. I had affidavits testifying that their father was absent and not consistent with child support. The judge awarded me full custody, which is unusual for New Mexico because this is a joint custody state. If the father were ever to question my ability as a parent, I have a strong history in the courts confirming me as the designated parent.

I think legislation that supports the gay and lesbian lifestyle is important. But I also think that education is essential. I try to be "out" whenever it's safe to be "out," because the more people who get to

My choice of sexual orientation certainly affects what and how I teach my children. I also have bi-racial children and that certainly affects my choices in terms of what I've had to confront and look at about our society — for instance what my kids bring home from school and how the educational system deals with different races (besides white, Anglo and European) historically and in the present. How families are portrayed is another issue, in books, movies and the educational system.

Because I have an alternative lifestyle and I have bi-racial children, I have influence in a lot of different areas because of the fact that I'm a parent and I'm out there working for my children and protecting them. For example, Josh is ten years old and he has "sexist" and "African-American" in his vocabulary. My alternative lifestyle has affected his language for dealing with the world and his perspective on dealing with difference.

I interact in the world and I am out, especially in my kids' schools with teachers and principals. Because of the fact that I'm active, it forces those people to deal with difference. I'm very honest and direct. I don't overlook the issues that have come up around race. I interview my children's teachers every year before I sign them up. Look, I'm a lesbian and I don't want my children in a classroom where that's

know me as credible in my profession, as a good mother and as a professional — in whatever sphere — they also know me as a lesbian. It balances out people's prejudices, ideas and stereotypes. Education on an individual basis and wide-scale sensitivity training must be done.

It's so complex. The laws on the books now that protect against discrimination give credibility to people who have the strength to fight. They have that safety net to say, "I was discriminated against on the basis of my sex or race." They have laws to protect them, but gay and lesbian people don't have that. For example, I think the Sharon Bottoms case was horrendous. Her child was taken away because we have these laws on the books that say being a lesbian is illegal. She had no basis on which to fight that case because according to Virginia's sodomy laws, she was breaking the law.

an issue, where they have to defend me because of my lifestyle and my choices.

I was in a long-term relationship for three years. The woman I was with made it clear she would be just a friend to my children. I won't ever do that again. I'm more inclined to try and scare women off by introducing my children as soon as possible. I was under a lot of stress all the time feeling I had to protect my lover from my children. Now it's understood: these are my appendages.

There are women in my children's lives who are committed to interacting with them. I go to great lengths to make sure they have women of color in their lives. I think that's important.

I'm glad that I had my children young for a lot of reasons. Now their growing independence meshes with my own independence. I don't have to interrupt my life now and have children.

I don't separate myself as a woman, as a lover, as a friend or as a parent. I don't need to.

"I'm glad that I had my children young for a lot of reasons. Now their growing independence meshes with my own independence. I don't have to interrupt my life now and have children."

KIM NICKEL-DUBIN, ALI NICKEL-DUBIN AND JORDAN
California

Kim and **Ali Nickel-Dubin** met at country-western two-step lessons at Club 22 in L.A. Now they live in an earth-toned condominium in North Hollywood with their two-and-a-half-month-old daughter, Jordan, cocker spaniel, "Playback," and two cats, "Paws" and "Reewynd." Kim is a 29-year-old pharmaceutical technician, and Ali is a 26-year-old marriage and family therapist and full-time homemaker. In 1987, Ali founded Just For Us, a local support group for children of gays and lesbians in L.A. and became the co-director of the national organization **COLAGE,** Children of Lesbians & Gays Everywhere. "My dad was gay," Ali said. "He passed away over two years ago. It's kind of sad because we're missing a grandfather who would be really involved and excited."

Kim: It has been difficult adjusting to our life with the baby, but the hardships have been totally overshadowed by the rewards.

Ali: On an average day, we wake up at 1:30 a.m. and I breastfeed Jordan. Hopefully she goes right to sleep until 6 a.m. Then she gets up and nurses again and goes to sleep. Kim's alarm used to wake the baby and me right after we'd gone back to sleep. Now I just roll over and hit her and say, "I've just gone to sleep. Wake up!"

Kim: That usually works. I have an hour drive each way to work and get home at 6:30 p.m.

Ali: When she comes home, I want to say, "Here, take the baby!" That's the hardest part of our day. Kim comes home from work and she's exhausted and I've had the baby all day and I'm exhausted. Kim needs to relax and wants to eat dinner.

Kim: Since we've discovered that, we've been working on that transition.

Ali: Twice a week, Jordan and I go to "Mommy and Me." It's a support group of 25 to 30 moms and their babies who meet at the hospital up the street. I'm bringing Kim with me next Tuesday for the first time. That's kind of scary. I would imagine they're all straight.

Kim: What's been interesting is that Ali has always been so "out." Once she got pregnant and was starting to show, she went back into the closet a little bit. Here I am, proud that she's pregnant, and all of a sudden, she's like, "Well, we don't need to advertise it."

Ali: I don't know what it was. I've been very "out" and proud to be a mom and proud to be a lesbian, but I don't like being judged and I don't want Jordan judged because of me. Having been raised by a gay dad, I know it really doesn't change anything. In fact, it made me a way more open-minded and tolerant person and proud of who I am.

A lot of people say, "How do you plan on telling Jordan and raising her as a child of two women?" I want to respond, "Well, when did your parents tell you they were straight?"

Kim: We want to be recognized and have the same privileges that any other parent has — it's something to be celebrated and not looked down upon.

athy Peterman lives on the Wisconsin-Minnesota border with her two-year-old twin daughters, Adrianne and Morganne. The sky filled with purple clouds as we drove out through miles of cornfields and past an old drive-in. After we arrived and had dinner together, the girls chased outside, in and around the tall grass sparkling with fireflies. After laying them down on Pocahontas and Lion King pillows, Kathy sat down to tell us about her life as an executive for American Express and a single mother of twins.

I was born in Barberton, Ohio, in 1958. I grew up in Norton, Ohio, which is right beside Barberton. My paternal grandparents were German-speaking Hungarians and my maternal grandparents were Pennsylvania Dutch. So I'm pretty much as German as they come. I was raised United Methodist — a nice, liberal, socially focused church. We prayed for the success of the high school football team — we weren't trying to save America or redeem our souls.

I'm the oldest of four girls. We lived in one house our entire life which my parents still own and still live in. I had a very blue-collar, all-American life. Saturday nights, you killed a chicken, you put vaseline on your patent-leather shoes, you took a bath, you ate a bowl of popcorn and split one 16-ounce bottle of RC cola with your three other sisters. That's how life was. I was always a kind of scrawny kid with a bunch of allergies. I stuttered probably to keep from having to talk to people because I think I knew at a very early age that I was different.

I did my undergraduate degree at the University of Akron back in the days when it wasn't popular to study accounting. I got accosted in the halls by the boys and told that I had scored too high on the tests, that I was just going to marry someone and raise kids and it wasn't really necessary to get high marks. I just knew that when I got done with that accounting degree, I couldn't be an accountant — much too boring. I decided to pursue my other passion — computers — and I came to the University of Minnesota because they had a great program in Management Information Systems. So I was a 22-year-old MBA ready to make my mark on the world.

Usually I say I prefer same-sex relationships and I just leave it at that. I don't exclude it as a life possibility — that I might some day be with a guy — I just can't imagine it. It gives me the willies. Learning that I was lesbian was the most wonderful thing that ever happened to me because finally everything made sense. I didn't have to stutter anymore. I wasn't embarrassed about who I was. I didn't feel odd. It's been one of the most calming, centering, congruent things that ever happened to me.

I always knew I'd have children. I never expected to have a partner. I never made that a criterion. I had set age 35 as a target. I pre-negotiated my support arrangements; it was a really good experience for me to go talk to people who were part of my life and say, "This is really part of my plan. I'm going to do this."

I got very mixed results. My 83-year old neighbor, straight as an arrow, said, "You have my unconditional support. You'll be the most wonderful mother in the world. If anyone around here is concerned that you've been inseminated, you send them to me."

I got pregnant in November, so I got to tell my family over Christmas and they did really well. My father said, "Do you know what you're doing? And I said, "Dad, I've done more research, more reading,

> **Saturday nights, you killed a chicken, you put vaseline on your patent-leather shoes, you took a bath, you ate a bowl of popcorn and split one 16-ounce bottle of RC cola with your three other sisters. That's how life was.**

you're there because you see that if you aren't, they quickly begin to decline.

I played Kenny G. for them and Barbra Streisand and k.d. lang and the Brandenburg concertos. I talked incessantly about all of the planets, the United States, the state of Minnesota, my life and every job I ever had. Their souls were there from the beginning. Their eyes were fused shut and their fingers had no nails and they were shriveled and scrawny, but there was a spirit there that was afraid. I could see it. Wouldn't you want to hear your mom? Wouldn't you want to know you could do it?

The secondary focus was definitely on me. I needed to make milk. That was the only thing that I could do for them directly. So my friend the electric breast pump and I had seven rounds every day. By the time they got home, I had 144 cartons of milk inventoried.

There is no down time in this house. There is a routine. If that dishwasher doesn't get set to go off when I go to sleep tonight, tomorrow is screwed from the beginning. I mean, it's just that simple. If those clothes that they had on from today and my clothes don't go in a pile and if one load of laundry doesn't go in before my head lays on the pillow, we start tomorrow behind. If the garbage doesn't go in the garbage cans and those cans don't go on the back of my Subaru, we start tomorrow behind.

Every family needs a lesbian. I'm guessing every family has one, they just don't know or acknowledge it. Some day they will. God knew that Newt Gingrich needed a lesbian sister and I'm betting Jerry Falwell has one and Pat Robertson has one, too.

> **There is no down time in this house. There is a routine. If that dishwasher doesn't get set to go off when I go to sleep tonight, tomorrow is screwed from the beginning.**

more planning, more preparation than any mother you will ever meet in the world, but I will not sit here and tell you that I know what I'm doing. But I'm really excited." He got up and gave me a big hug.

I had one of those romantic births: 18 people in the room, stripped naked, velcroed to a table, arms straight out, feet up in the stirrups, with two perinatologists, who are the most specialized of baby deliverers. They do purely multiple births, hazardous births and preemie births. The girls were delivered at 26 weeks. Adrianne was a tough little cookie. She was up and out at 1 lb., 10 oz. and Morganne was 1 lb., 14 oz.

Preemie life is an odyssey. Adrianne was hospitalized for 83 days and Morganne for 88 days. It's a very hard period because their health is very volatile. You're very focused on their well-being and being calm when

They have an annual Valentine's Day singles dance here. I was just amazed that during that entire evening, when I would meet women and say I hadn't been out dancing in a while because I had twins, they would just turn and walk away. I honestly believe I would have had more dates if I were a straight, single mother with twins. The women I have dated since the girls were born want more attention focused on them than I would ever be able to give. I would like to find a partner who could share in guiding Morganne and Adrianne into the future. Someone who loves them as I do and who could watch them grow.

Jashe Kurland is a 30-year-old massage therapist of Eastern European Jewish ancestry. Her 31-year-old partner, Terri Grover, is a graphic designer of mixed German, Scots, Irish and English heritage. They met seven years ago and adopted their two-year-old daughter, Willa, who was eating blue corn chips, pushing her lawnmower and blowing bubbles the afternoon we were there. Speaking both Chinese and English, Willa practiced saying "spaghetti" and "cheese" as we took her picture underneath the cerulean blue New Mexico sky. Their four dogs, "Toma," "Mishe," "Hana," and "P.J.," and their orange cat, "Ruben," occasionally joined them for their portraits.

Terri: About three years ago, Tashe was trying to get pregnant for a while using a sperm bank and it wasn't working. Then we decided to ask my brother and he was very excited about being the donor. We inseminated twice with him. The first time, Tashe got pregnant and nine weeks later, she miscarried. It was intense.

Tashe: After I miscarried, we waited a couple months and tried again.

Terri: She was getting really stressed out that she wasn't pregnant and started feeling bad about herself. I said, "We're ready for a baby. Why don't we adopt one?" We were ready to start a family and I knew there were plenty of babies out there.

Tashe: At that time, we heard about these little girls in China.

Terri: A friend of Tashe's mother had just adopted a baby from China. I have always felt an affinity to Chinese culture. I thought this could be a really incredible opportunity for us to adopt a child.

Tashe: So I applied to an agency as a single parent. It took four months of completing paperwork, and then the papers went to China to be translated. It was two months from the time all the papers were submitted until we got this very small picture of Willa.

We got a phone call that said you're getting a little girl out of Xin Jiang province. She was the very first baby to be adopted out of this Northwest province.

Terri: We were really excited. We both bonded immediately to her picture.

Tashe: She was actually at that point in an orphanage. She had been with a foster mother for 17 months and then she went to the orphanage.

Our agency said her name is Li Meizhen and they were all worried that we'd say we didn't want her because she was 18 months old. I didn't hesitate at all. We just knew she was the right baby for us. After we got her picture, we waited two months before they said that we could come and get her. It was really hard to wait for our travel date.

" I wrapped her up and sat her down on my lap and she just relaxed into my arms. That was the greatest feeling. **"**

We spent all of our time making copies of her picture and sending it all over the country to all of our families. Our families have been really involved in this from the beginning and really excited about it. Finally, we flew into Beijing on a Friday and then into Xin Jiang province and then to the capital city, Urumqi.

Terri: We went to dinner at this restaurant and then we took the elevator up to our floor in the hotel.

Tashe: When the elevator doors opened, she was standing there, holding this woman's hand. She was wearing thick layers of all these clothes. Her pants were these military jacket sleeves which had been cut off and sewn into these split bottom pants.

Terri: She looked like a little snowman.

Tashe: So sturdy. With a fat, round face.

Terri: Her hair was shaved like a bowl cut. She looked like a little boy.

Tashe: I knelt down to say "hi" to her. The Chinese women were saying, "This is your mama." They wanted to give her a bath that evening and when she came out of the tub was actually the first time I got to hold her. She was screaming hysterically. I wrapped her up and sat her down on my lap and she just relaxed into my arms. That was the greatest feeling.

Terri: She was potty-trained already, but they took her into the hallway and she squatted and went in the hallway on the rug. She was terrified of the bathroom. She wouldn't go near it. When we first brought her home, she was terrified of the animals, especially the cat. She would freak out whenever she saw the cat. She thought it was a rodent or something.

Tashe: She watched everything so carefully, what we did, what we were saying. The first couple days all she would do was stand next to us. After about a week she was walking around. The first English word she used was "baby." She knew she was the *baby*.

Terri: She's so sharp. You can say something once and she remembers it three days later. She makes a lot of jokes. She's got a really good sense of humor. I've never met anyone her age who makes jokes the way she does. A month after we were home, we were doing something in the yard on the grass and she farted. I said, "What was that?" And she said, "Music!" Then she laughs because she thinks it's funny.

Tashe: I love just watching her run around the house. She can get out of bed now by herself. She was wearing this little T-shirt with no pants on when she was napping the other day. She climbed out of bed and went running down the hallway. As I saw her running, I just thought, "It's so incredible that she lives here in our house with us and she's our baby."

Juin Charnell has one pierced eyebrow and cropped-short hair. She is a 34-year-old freelance writer, performance artist and single mother of four children, Jenna (11), Jade (9), Joi (8) and Justin (5). It was a muggy July morning in Ruby's Cafe, a local breakfast hang-out, when we picked up an issue of *Minnesota Women's Press* and read Juin's story titled "Family Gathering." It inspired us to contact her, and later that week, Juin and her children came to our hotel and sat quietly on the bed while she told her story.

I was born in France in 1962. I can trace my roots as far back as Louisiana because that's where my grandmother was from and where my mother was born. When I grew up, we were Baptist, African Methodist Episcopalians, and we went to Lutheran churches and sanctified churches. Ethnically, I am a black person in America.

I don't mind the word "lesbian." But it's so long — les-bi-an. Usually I just say "dyke." When you say "gay," everyone automatically thinks men. I love "dyke" because I'm a strong woman and that typifies a strong woman. I would have labeled myself much earlier in life, except I didn't know any other lesbians, other than the women I was dating. We didn't know what to call ourselves. We were just women who dated women.

Although I wanted six kids, I never wanted to be married to any man. But I didn't know how not to be married. My grandmother or my mother would have killed me. You did not have kids illegitimately. So I got married, had kids and got my divorces as quickly as I could.

I loved being pregnant with all of my kids because I thought I was most beautiful then. I cherished giving birth to all of them. Now I think some of the best times we have are when we get in my bed and we're talking.

The hardest thing about being a single lesbian mom is that women assume I want someone to co-parent. The only thing you have to be with my kids is a friend. It's the same thing I had to tell my second husband.

My responsibility as a parent is to make sure my kids are independent. The hardest part of that is if I tell them to challenge authority, they also want to challenge me. And that's a hard balance.

I like my kids to know what's going on in the world. I want them to go as far and high as they can possibly go. I don't want them to be limited by the color of their skin. But I'll also let them know that other people will try to hold them back because they're black.

In my neighborhood, we're the only queer family and we're the only black family. Everyone else just goes along. They're not worried about their civil rights, because their civil rights are not at stake at the moment.

Prejudice is not allowed in our schools. One day, some kids were doing gay and racist jokes. The teacher's way of dealing with it was, "Okay, be quiet, don't bring it up again." I told them, "No, that doesn't do it: I'll come and teach a workshop for your class on homophobia." You can't wait until the kids are in the fourth or fifth grades. Teaching tolerance has to start early.

> "Although I wanted six kids, I never wanted to be married to any man. But I didn't know how not to be married. My grandmother or my mother would have killed me."

MALKA GOLDEN-WOLFE AND BARBARA ZACKY WITH DAUGHTERS ALEXANDRA AND CYNTHIA, SON-IN-LAW MARQUE AND GRANDCHILDREN REMY, NICKY AND JESSICA
Arizona

Malka Golden-Wolfe is a psychotherapist, an advanced clinical hypnotherapist, psychic and artist. She and her partner, Barbara Zacky, run Paradise Ranch; the Sedona Children's and Elder's Project; the International Council of Crones and Grandmothers; and the New Realities Institute. They live on a ranch nestled between cinnamon- and cayenne-colored rocks with their Akita "Mudgie Kiwi," also known as "Spiritkeeper of the West." Malka's daughters Alexandra (38) and Cynthia (36), son-in-law Marque (37) and grandchildren Jessica (8), Remy (4) and Nicky (1 1/2) gathered on their deck for the afternoon. Malka's son Michael (33), his wife Janet and their four children live in Washington state and are not pictured here.

I was born on September 25, 1942, in Los Angeles, at 7:03 a.m. I am a double Libra moon in Aries. I'm a first-generation Russian-Austrian Jew. My father was born in a small town right on the Ukranian border called Poltava. My mother's family came from Vienna, Austria.

> **In the generation I grew up in, women were not offered any choices. The focus was girls got married and had children in order to be normal and fulfilled.**

I had my first experience with a woman when I was 18 and eight months pregnant with my second daughter. I had given my first daughter, Alexandra, up for adoption when I was 15. I've had three husbands, starting with the father of Cynthia and Michael when I was 16.

In the generation I grew up in, women were not offered any choices. The focus was girls got married and had children in order to be normal and fulfilled. Today, it's totally incredible that women have choices, with all the focus on lifestyle options, women now have support to make other choices. It's really incredible that women have found the freedom to live with women and make a conscious choice to have children.

I was cumulatively married for 23 years. I stopped marrying men in 1978. All during these years, I thought of myself as a bisexual woman. I came to believe there was no such thing as a straight woman. I slept with so many of my "straight" women friends, I should have gotten some kind of award. I used to take the kids camping with one friend of mine. She would take her kids and I would take mine. We'd leave the husbands at home and get it on in the mountains outside of L.A.

I have the most wonderful, supportive, loving children that any mother could pray for. If you were sitting down with a paper and pencil designing the kids of your dreams, you couldn't design better kids than I have. I think the secret to my kids loving and respecting me is that I have never been fake with them.

❝I really wanted him to know that our relationship was not out of the ordinary, even though it is not part of the majority. As he grows up, I'm hoping he's one voice in accepting all paths and choices for all people.❞

I've accepted them for who they are. If we are judgmental with kids, then we'll end up with kids who judge us.

My unconditional love for them has allowed me to be more inclusive and let go of ideas that might separate me from them. I think they've done the same for me. Our love for each other has been the dominating force in our lives. Because even when I had all those husbands, I used to say, "It's me and my kids." Even when I was getting divorced, I never felt alone. I had my kids and they had me.

One thing I've learned is to allow them to make their own mistakes. Let them experience the consequences of, let's say, poor financial choices. I can listen empathetically and, in most cases, I identify with them. They are very much like me. I have tried to guide them by telling them "Don't do what your mother did." But if they do, they do. And I support and love them.

The other thing I feel proud about is that I never divided them from their father. So they have a wonderful relationship with their biological father and I do too. He's my oldest friend. Even when we were divorced, we always shared the decision-making with the kids.

I could go out and "pass" in the world as a heterosexual woman. I wear dresses and have naturally curly hair. People wouldn't look at me and say, "That woman must be a lesbian!" I could pass in the world if I wanted to. But I feel that every woman who doesn't come out makes it harder for the next woman to be out of the closet in the world. If we want a world that encompasses everyone, then we must make it happen by saying, "Here I am. I'm a lesbian and I'm normal."

Being a grandmother is the best! I feel like I have to teach my grandchildren to be the kind of people I want to see populating the planet. I'm very conscious of wanting a big place in their hearts, minds and lives.

One summer Barbara and I took the grandchildren on a vacation. When we were driving through Yellowstone park, my grandson Jonathan — who was five then — said to the man at the gate, "They're married!" pointing to me and Barbara. I didn't say anything about it until we were sitting down to dinner. I said, "Tell me, Jonathan, when you and Mommy and Daddy go some place, do you tell the waitress that your mom and dad are married?" "No," he said. "I'm wondering why you did that with Grandma Barbara and me? There's nothing more unusual about us being married than Mommy and Daddy being married." He thought about it for a minute and said, "Okay. You're right." I really wanted him to know that our relationship was not out of the ordinary, even though it is not part of the majority. As he grows up, I'm hoping he's one voice in accepting all paths and choices for all people.

For my children and grandchildren, I wish life for them on a healthy planet, where the air is clean and the waters are not polluted, where women are nurtured and respected and revered. I hope that they understand the Divine as the Great Mother who gives and sustains life. I hope that they understand the male and female energies within themselves regardless of what gender they are, that they respect other humans, that they make a positive contribution toward a better society.

KRIS MELYCHER, HEIDI GRIGGS AND RIVER
California

e walked up a block where bird-of-paradise and cypress grew on front lawns and lots of kids were playing in driveways. Four-year-old River was sitting on the sidewalk outside his house, playing with his truck and lawnmower on a Wednesday afternoon. His mother, Heidi Griggs, a 28-year-old "mostly Italian" hospital nutritionist, had just come home from work. Her partner, 34-year-old Kris Melycher, is River's co-parent and had just returned from her job as a cook. While we interviewed Heidi, River's father Ray Drew dropped by and played Legos with him. Ray is the 35-year-old director of GLPCI, the Gay & Lesbian Parents Coalition International, and shares custody of River with Heidi, who told us how River came to live with them.

My older sister called me in 1993, right after River was born, and said she was having a hard time. River was only two months old then. She has a total of five kids now, two live with my father and two live with her on the streets primarily or in homeless shelters.

I totally love my sister. I just wanted to take her and save her. She's a really good person, but she's a product of her environment. I have a tremendous amount of respect for her, but I was fortunate enough to have mentors all my life, outside of my family. We live in different worlds.

I got on a plane and went out to Kansas City. When I got there, her house was filled with smoke. They had given River adult Nyquil and blown pot smoke in his face. He had diaper rash so bad, his skin almost came off in his diaper. When I took him to the hospital, they were going to arrest me for child abuse. I said, "I'm not his mom." They started talking about all kinds of legal stuff that was going to happen, and it seemed easier for me to take him and take care of him. That night I brought him back to my house in San Francisco.

At that time, I lived in a studio with a futon, a waterbed, my music equipment and a dyke poster. I was the average San Francisco hard-core dyke. I knew nothing about kids, particularly a two-month old. So I laid him down on the waterbed and got a doctor for emergency medical care. River was a chronic asthmatic and needed medication. The doctor came to our house almost every night and taught me how to bathe him, give him his inhaler, what temperature his bottle should be and what he should be eating.

It was scary because I knew my whole life was going to change. After I got permanent guardianship, I was accepting responsibility and thinking about what kind of family I could give to him. The whole reason I decided not to have kids was that I didn't agree with the kind of parenting I was raised with. It forced me to look at my family history and remember it, in order not to repeat it.

When I came to San Diego, I met Kris, who's his stepmom and co-parent now. I was seeking a father for River at that time and met Ray Drew who was running the "Considering Parenthood" group. It was important to me that River have a father and male figure in his life, maybe because I didn't grow up with my mother. I grew up with just my dad.

My adoption is final this month and then Ray will start his. River has been a ward of the state since I got him four years ago. At this point, I'm the only person he knows as "Mom." I'm the only person that's consistently been in his life since he was two months old. And it's been so good!

> **They had given River adult Nyquil and blown pot smoke in his face. He had diaper rash so bad, his skin almost came off in his diaper.**

"When Evan was born, he was put into my arms. He was big, over nine pounds. It was the most amazing thing because I couldn't relate to him at all."

oy Tomchin lives with her three-year-old son Evan in a lavish, tri-level penthouse with a view of the Hudson River from her living room. Evan's first finger paintings, framed in gold, hang on the dining room wall and he plays with his toy motorcycle in a burgundy velvet chair. A 50-year-old real estate developer of Russian/Jewish heritage, Joy is a prominent figure and political activist in New York City's lesbian and gay community. After her interview, Joy brought Evan on his bicycle down Hudson Street as 3,000 cyclists were finishing the Tanqueray AIDS Ride from Boston to New York. We all stood on the corner together as a stream of red, yellow and orange shirts, bikes and helmets flew by.

I wanted to have children my entire life. But for many years, I felt that it wouldn't work because I was gay and I didn't think I could do it alone. As I got older, I craved a relationship where we could have children together. I had a couple of relationships with women who had children. They weren't great relationships, but my connections with the kids were great. Finally I decided to do it alone.

I was 47 when Evan was born. His surrogate mother is a lesbian mother of two in Missouri. I met her and her kids and immediately liked her. She's just a doll, a very sweet and wonderful person. She's a registered nurse and loves being pregnant.

I signed a contract with her that I would adopt Evan at birth. I flew to Missouri and picked her up and we drove to Hot Springs, Arkansas, two weeks before she was due. We went to Arkansas to have the baby because adoption laws in Arkansas are the best in the country. It only takes 30 days for a final adoption; in New York, it takes a year and a half.

I had to declare residency in Arkansas, so I rented an apartment for 30 days. We did a tour of their new medical center and it was amazing. It was a Catholic hospital and the nurse who gave us the tour was a nun. She said, "We know exactly what's going on. We know you're lesbians and we know it's a surrogate birth. You won't have any problems here. We're a Catholic hospital and we believe in freedom." They couldn't have been nicer to us.

When Evan was born, he was put into my arms. He was big, over nine pounds. It was the most amazing thing because I couldn't relate to him at all. He was screaming and kind of cute, but I had no feeling for him at all. I thought, aren't you supposed to feel immediate love for this baby? So there I was, by myself, in the middle of Hot Springs, Arkansas with this little infant for two weeks, while the judge took care of the papers. But by the end of the two weeks, I had this intense overwhelming love for him.

For the first two years, I took him to work with me two days a week. The first six months were easy because he'd wake up, eat and go back to sleep. Everybody in the office loved him and played with him. He had a little section in my office with a lot of toys and there was a playground across the street. He'd sit by the elevator and watch people come in and out. It was really fun. People would come to the office to conduct business and then they'd see this little guy sitting on the floor and it would change everything. They'd relax, smile, laugh and play.

People used to say to me, "I just can't picture you as a mother." I didn't find that insulting. But some friends said, "What is he going to call you? Mommy?" They'd laugh and think it was the funniest thing they ever heard. That hurt. Because I'm butch, they thought

hope that he doesn't think it's a big deal. I personally think that it's possible to make that a strength in our relationship rather than something that's harmful.

My strongest goal is that he be gentle because he's big and he's a boy. He's bigger than all his friends and when he tries to hug them, he knocks them right over. I try to teach him a lot but he learns and masters much of his world on his own.

Now people say, "It seems like you and Evan have been together forever." In the morning, he gets up and climbs into bed with me. We cuddle and fall back asleep together. I love that. He squeezes my neck and kisses me. Also, he dresses exactly like me. We have the same belts and the same shoes. We wear the same sneakers. When I put my black belt on in the morning, he runs and gets his belt. I'm totally in love with this little guy.

I somehow couldn't raise a child, feed him and change diapers and get up in the middle of the night. Even women in the gay community thought it was a bad idea. I felt they were confronting me with stereotypes about what it means to be butch.

At some point, Evan will have to deal with the facts that he has a gay mother and he's adopted. I

> **My strongest goal is that he be gentle because he's big and he's a boy. He's bigger than all his friends and when he tries to hug them, he knocks them right over.**

We flew over the Willamette River and deep green diamonds of earth into the Eugene airport. It was raining when we arrived; a flock of geese flew overhead as we made our way to the rent-a-car. When we pulled into Christine Frazer's driveway in the late afternoon, the rain finally stopped. She had the hoods up on two cars and was just getting over a cold. Although currently a software specialist, Christine worked as an auto mechanic for 20 years and raised her 26-year-old daughter Juniper as a single parent. A tall woman with "Castilian Spanish and good ol' Okie American" roots, Christine called her grown daughter "my bambino."

I came out when I was 19 years old, wandering through New Mexico as a pregnant hippie chick. I met a woman I knew right away was a lesbian. We were together six months, then right after the baby was born, she left. I was devastated and it was horrible. My son was born in August and I shut down. I said I would never love a woman again.

I met Juniper's father at a commune. Jasper and I were married, but I never felt like I grasped the institution of marriage. It's not like we had a formal wedding. We got married in the judge's chambers and I was wearing jeans. Just a couple months after we were together, there was a fire in the commune and my baby son died. That was pretty rough.

I have a very strong tigress feeling about being a mom. It changed me. I was a happy peacenik chick trying to do the peace-love thing and turn the other cheek. When I had my son, I was like a tiger with a cub. I would kill you and pull out your eyeballs if you threatened my child in any way. It was a very radical change.

Juniper was born in a cabin in 1971 in Dexter, Oregon. Jasper got sick with lymph cancer right after. We fought it for about a year, and when he died, she was 13 months old. We didn't have any electricity or running water and with him being so ill, rural living got to be too hard. When I look back on it over the years, I wouldn't wish this on anyone — to lose a friend and lover and a son. But I had to look back at certain points and say, "Well, I'm lucky probably. Other people have had it worse."

Juniper and I moved into town eventually. It was hard having a kid at that time. There weren't a lot of other lesbian mothers around, but Juniper grew up in a very supportive and growing community of lesbians and friends. She grew up seeing a lot of strong women role models.

I worked on cars for close to 20 years. My first lesson as a mechanic was when I drove to New Mexico and an axle bearing went out. I had to learn to fix that on the road. I learned by "have-to-do." I was a good mechanic, but it gets to you eventually. We were a struggling business serving poor people mostly. It's pretty hard to do well in that. I worked a lot of long, hard hours.

Juniper hung out with me at the shop when she was little. We didn't close until six, so she would come and sort nuts and bolts, so we could recycle them. She'd sort them by size. The next thing she learned was to sweep the shop floor and how to solvent-mop it. Then when she got older, she would add up all the parts receipts and file invoices. I think it helped her be responsible and made it easier when she was getting a job out in the world.

A joy of being a mother is having a daughter. When I get together with my mom and Juniper, it is really special. You see so much of the physical resemblance, of what's inherited. It's really great. I don't regret any of it.

Fifteen-month-old Jude was eating a banana and just learning how to hop on a hot July afternoon near the banks of the Rio Grande. A load of colorful wash hung on the line outside the straw bale house she shares with her moms, Jane Marx and Ilene Weiss, dog "Zoe" and "Muggins" the cat. Jane is a 41-year-old lawyer and second-generation Russian/German Jew born in Detroit. Ilene Weiss is a 41-year-old sign language interpreter born in the Bronx and a Russian/Romanian Jew. We watched Jane pitch a softball game the night before their interview and the next day were invited to go swimming with Jude in the courtyard pool.

Ilene: I was organizing a "Take Back the Night" march in 1985 and Jane was in law school. Someone told me she'd be a good person to bring leaflets to the law school. We knew of each other then. Four years after that, we met again at temple. It was high holy days and we started chatting.

Jane: We talked on the phone because I was traveling a lot. Then Ilene's father died suddenly.

Ilene: I went to L.A. for a few weeks because my dad had died and when I got back, Jane took off on another trip. I was so grief stricken at that time. I was torn up and was more emotionally open with her than I had been with other people.

Jane: Also, at that time, my partner Pat was diagnosed with lung cancer and died in the sixth month of her diagnosis.

Ilene: That's how we became a family — through Jane responding to my dad's death. Then when Jane's ex-lover was so sick, I decided to go through this with her and I became a caretaker of Pat.

Jane: After Pat died, I did some intense counseling and dealt with a lot of issues — the loss of Pat and a lot of childhood stuff. I started getting clearer about wanting to have a child. Then I was diagnosed with breast cancer. This was four years ago. Having a kid was on my mind and it certainly was one of the things I talked to the doctors about when I was trying to decide on what kind of treatment to receive.

I had surgery and radiation and now the breast cancer is gone. Periodically, I'd check in and ask my doctor if I was clear enough to pursue a pregnancy and also wondered whether my breast would produce milk. It wasn't an estrogen-responsive cancer, so eventually my doctor said, "If you're going to have a kid, now is a good time to do it."

Ilene: I was really ambivalent about becoming a parent, but I knew this was a major life decision for Jane.

Jane: We didn't make a classic joint decision to have a baby. Having cancer made it very clear to me what I wanted to do in my life. So I began looking at what a child needs to feel comfortable in the world. Ilene has a very good, old friend who is Jude's father. He's Jewish too — which is important — a Sephardic Jew. During this process, Ilene naturally became involved and eventually enthusiastic.

Ilene: My family was not very religious, but they were very culturally Jewish and Yiddish was spoken in the home. Sharing a cultural identity enhanced my relationship with

> **After Pat died, I did some intense counseling and dealt with a lot of issues — the loss of Pat and a lot of childhood stuff.**

> **Before Jude was conceived, we did a ceremony to invite her to come be with us. We invited her father and a few friends of ours. We all climbed up into the treehouse and brought different ceremonial things.**

Jane, so when we thought about creating a family, we wanted familiarity and cohesiveness.

Jane: Having a known dad was important to us and preferably he'd be someone who'd want to be involved in Jude's life.

Ilene: I've known her father for 15 years. When Jane got to know him a little bit, she said, "That's the dad!" He goes to the same temple where we met. He's a woodworker, scrupulously honest, creative and a good guy. He's someone Jude could go off with and we wouldn't be sitting home biting our fingernails.

Before Jude was conceived, we did a ceremony to invite her to come be with us. We invited her father and a few friends of ours. We all climbed up into the treehouse and brought different ceremonial things. Her father wrote a beautiful poem for her called "Craftsman's Daughter." It begins, "We'll bake bread together and sharpen Japanese chisels on waterstones.

We'll walk hand-in-hand to the bosque speaking Spanish. We'll plant watermelons every spring and spit the pits at the wall in the summer ..."

Jane: The ceremony was really about setting our intent and welcoming Jude into this world.

Ilene: Creating a space for her to come.

Jane: I feel like I became ripe to be pregnant then. She became very real to us. It wasn't long after that I got pregnant — the second time I inseminated. We did it at home. I'd tell her dad when I was about to ovulate and he'd meet us at the door with a little film canister and a piece of sage. He always had a little gift.

Ilene: Jude was born April 12, 1996, at 5:08 a.m. When she was born, we had a naming ceremony for her. The rabbi came to our house and we had people over. Part of that ceremony was welcoming her into her lineage of people — the Jews.

Jane: We both chose her name — Jude Elyana Marx. "Jude" is in memory of Ilene's father. "Elyana" is in memory of my grandfather whose Russian name was Elyaho.

Ilene: She calls Jane "Ma" and in the last few weeks, she's been saying "Ima" for me, which is Hebrew for mother. That was exciting when she called me "Ima."

Jane: If I ask myself what I need to do as a good parent, I would say to just let her know how much we love her, to encourage her to be all of who she is and to keep her safe.

CAROL FORSTER, ANA HOOVER AND JENNIFER

Arizona

C arol Forster and Ana Hoover have three grown children, Jeff (28), Dean (26) and Jennifer (23). Carol is a social worker of Norwegian-Swedish/English ancestry who was born in Los Angeles in 1947. Ana is an English/German "recovering fundamentalist" and police records clerk, born in Pittsfield, Illinois, in 1945. On the Saturday afternoon we arrived, Carol was wearing lavender Birkenstocks and coral toenail polish and lipstick. "Maya," their desert dog, "rescued from death row," scampered about.

Ana: I grew up in a town of 350 people. The general mentality seemed to be, "Well, you didn't educate your breeding animals, so why would you educate your women?" I went to secretarial school, biding time until I got married at age 22. My husband was a livestock feed salesman and was transferred to a plant in a small town in northern Illinois. We bought a house there and as soon as the house next door was finished, you'll never guess who moved in. The new minister at the Lutheran church — Carol!

Carol: I moved in right after I was ordained in 1982. I was a single parent with two kids and just out of the seminary in Chicago. I was assigned to this parish of Swedish farmers out in the middle of nowhere.

Ana: At that time, I was recovering from a hysterectomy. We became friends and I began going over at night to visit Carol after her kids went to bed. We'd sit at the dining room table and talk and in those days — chain smoke and drink Chablis.

Carol: I felt so isolated, away from all of my friends in Chicago. I really needed someone to talk to, and Annie was there for me.

Ana: Then one weekend, Carol went with me to see my grandmother to lend support. I hadn't been able to force myself to visit the nursing home where she had gone to live. She wasn't herself after my dad died. She depended on him and when he died, it was the worst thing in the world. Carol said, "I get two Sundays off a year. If I go with you, do you think you can do it?" I was so scared. When we walked into the nursing home, an aide was feeding my grandmother. I took the spoon and said, "Grandmother, do you know who this is?" She said, "Yes, it's Ana Lee." I knew that everything was going to be okay.

After we went to the nursing home together, we drove across the river into Hannibal, Missouri, and sat at a look-out point. It was a spiritual day for me. There were signs everywhere that God had worked through Carol and allowed me to be with my grandmother. On the way to my mother's house, there was a beautiful sunset. We took my mother with us and ate fish at the Barefoot Bar. That night, we slept in my mother's queen-size bed and said our "goodnights." I thanked Carol for going with me and leaned over and kissed her. I said, "Oh god, I'm sorry. Oh my gosh, I kissed the pastor right on the mouth! I can't believe I did that."

Carol: Then I said, "Hey, I kissed you back, remember?"

Ana: "Oh hell," I thought. "What does that mean? That's almost worse." The next day I took her to my favorite place on earth — the bluffs between the Illinois and the Mississippi rivers. We walked through the cattle and down into the woods and sat on a log. We admitted to each other we were in love. I felt like I found what I always thought I'd never find.

Carol: It was very scary for me. My kids were still in school, and our relationship was not compatible with my position in the church. We had a long way to go. We talked about this a lot and really struggled with it.

Ana: My relationship with my husband had been emotionally destructive for a long time, so I finally settled into our basement, quit my job and enrolled in college full-time. Two years later Carol loaned me $200 for the retainer for the attorney and I filed for divorce.

Carol: We've had some god-awful times and really great times since then. But Annie's always been there for me. When we told the kids about our relationship, we took Jennifer to the Dairy Queen and she was eating a Peanut Buster parfait. I said, "We really love each other." She said, "I know," and just kept eating her ice cream. She never missed a spoonful. We have been totally accepted by the kids.

Ana: We got close to each other's kids out of necessity — by helping each other out. Carol always took Jeff to his dentist appointments because as a pastor, her schedule was more flexible than mine. When we told Jeff about our relationship, we were driving back from the airport and he was in the back seat talking a mile a minute. I said, "Carol and I will continue living together. I love her, Jeff. I am in love with her." He reached between the bucket seats and said, "I love her too Mom." And that was it. We feel lucky to have kids who are happy, successful, have accepted us and have lives of their own. We also made it through their periods of normal teenage anger and rebellion. Now, we're going to be grandmothers! Hearing my son say that was a terrific moment. We're definitely proud of all of them.

In 1995, we had our commitment ceremony. We wrote the whole service together and had all the people who support us there. When we left the altar, our kids walked together behind us. We wanted that to be symbolic — after we were joined — that they literally and figuratively walk behind us. Later, when we were at the reception, Dean came over and gave Carol a big hug and kiss. Then he put his arm around me. He was hugging us both around the neck and said, "It's about time you guys did this!"

Carol and I have always thought that if you believe that love comes from God, how can you not believe that it's okay to love someone of the same sex? When I was married to a man, everything was acceptable. Now, I'm married to this good woman — and I am grateful for her being in my life.

"My kids were still in school, and our relationship was not compatible with my position in the church. We had a long way to go."

*J*anie Oakes has short spiked hair, freckles and a slight southern accent. She is a philanthropist and artist and lives with her 15-year-old daughter Amelia and a schnauzer named "Cloudy." Hollyhocks and sage were in full-bloom in her yard when we arrived in mid-July. As we sat under the back portal, drinking lemonade, Amelia came in wearing a black and white printed sleeveless dress, ready for photos. Later she changed into slouchy jeans with holes in the knees and a velour top. She talked about "heroin chic" and mocked its aesthetic during the rest of the photo session.

I was born in Wichita Falls, Texas, in 1946. I grew up in the Episcopal church and I am quite a Wasp. I shouldn't say I'm a Wasp because there are Russian Jews on my mother's side of the family. The story goes that my great-great-grandmother literally walked out of Russia with her jewels sewn into the seams of her clothing, leading a child by the hand. That Jewish thread is intriguing, especially since my daughter has recently become interested in Judaism.

All of my strong childhood memories are of women. The most significant woman was one of my mother's closest friends. She seemed to have such a remarkable mind and was very opinionated and very strong. When I was in high school, her husband died and she started working as the entertainment editor for the newspaper. She got tickets to everything and took me to a lot of events. When we went to the stock car races in the middle of summer in Amarillo, Texas, she wore a suit and alligator shoes and had her steno pad on her lap as we sat on these bleachers with grit in our eyes. There was this unbelievable sound of these cars screaming around. It seemed hilarious to me that we could go together to the stock car races, the symphony, or the opening of "Lawrence of Arabia."

I got married in 1970 and Amelia was born in 1982. I graduated from the University of Texas in 1970 with a degree in art. Later I went to nursing school and became an R.N. When I got pregnant, I had been a labor and delivery nurse and a nursing supervisor for a couple of years. Amelia was born in the hospital where I had worked in Oklahoma.

I went into labor on the Saturday before Easter. That night my husband and I were playing dominos and about 10:30 p.m. my friend Margee came over and said, "Oh yeah. You're moving right along." About two in the morning she said, "We need to go to the hospital." I said, "Oh I don't think so." She said, "Yes. It's time." So, she, Lane and I went. We got to the hospital and all the lights were off in the six labor rooms. All of the nurses were in the postpartum area. So Margee pushed me in a wheelchair and we turned on the lights and picked out a room we liked. Four hours later with her father present, Amelia was delivered by forceps without much anesthesia because nothing worked. It was still a great delivery and Amelia was very alert and awake.

I had rooming-in and the nurses from the nursery would come in to check on Amelia. They would say, "Do you have that baby in the bed with you again?" Because I hardly ever put her in the bassinet, I would say, "No, I have her in the bed with me *still.*"

Amelia was in a Montessori school from pre-school through the fourth grade. Her teachers were very sensitive to making sure that the children were exposed to all kinds of ideas. They got the whole range of ideas about creation, different kinds of families and belief systems.

> **One of the most important things about parenting is to be honest. You can't talk about honesty and then not be honest. Children always know the truth anyway.**

Her school community was an enormous support for all of us during the divorce and coming out process.

When I got involved with the woman who became my partner for four years, Amelia didn't ask any questions, and after several months, we began to wonder when she *would* ask. One day, when she was nine, she asked if we were lesbians. I said, "What does that word mean to you? What do you know about lesbians?" She answered, "I think they're people who like to garden." We said, "Well, not exactly." By the end of the conversation, Amelia had planned a wedding for us.

When Amelia was in the sixth grade, I organized a mother-daughter slumber party. Five girls, who had known each other since pre-school and their moms, spent the night at our house. Each girl was asked to invite one other significant woman in her life to share part of the evening. We ate pizza and then created a shrine made from objects each of us had brought. Then each Mom gave each girl a small gift. I gave a little silver milagros of open hands to express possibility and generosity. The gifts went into special amulet bags. The rest of the evening was just fun for everyone.

I'll tell you something I love to do with Amelia. I love to dye her hair. The first time was on the eve of her first day at camp. She was nine and she chose an intense shade of fuschia. I remember the color matched her shorts. Since then, I have been in on numerous hair-coloring projects. When she is leaning over the kitchen sink and I am standing there wearing rubber gloves, covering her thick, auburn hair with some amazing color, I think back fifteen years when her whole body fit in the kitchen sink.

My responsibility as a parent is to recognize that Amelia has her own unique path. I am here to guide and protect her as well as I can. The most difficult part of being a parent is letting children make their own mistakes. I have as much trouble with that as the next parent. One of the most important things about parenting is to be honest. You can't talk about honesty and then not be honest. Children always know the truth anyway.

I hope Amelia truly values and honors herself, and that she always seeks and speaks the truth. I wish for her to find a passion for something so compelling that she *must* learn it and do it. I hope she continues to develop deep connections to people and places. I hope that she always, all her life, loves to learn and that she is fortunate enough to find work or avocations that feed her soul. I pray that she is surrounded by compassion and love.

> "One day, when she was nine, she asked if we were lesbians. I said, 'What does that word mean to you? What do you know about lesbians?' She answered, 'I think they're people who like to garden.'"

CATHERINE SAALFIELD, MELANIE HOPE AND SADIE RAIN
New York

Catherine Saalfield and Melanie Hope live in a spacious SoHo loft with their three-month-old daughter Sadie Rain. Catherine is a 32-year-old film and videomaker, writer and teacher of German/French descent. Melanie is a 31-year-old poet and playwright with Caribbean roots. In early spring, we sat in their living room on a brown leather couch surrounded by books, African masks, orchids and an upright piano. Their "rescued-from-the-pound" dog "Boonji" and calico cat "Bella" wandered in and around the living room. In Sadie's room, an owl painting hung above her crib and a small stuffed giraffe stood nearby.

Melanie: We both knew we always wanted to have kids, so when we first met as friends, we talked about raising our kids together. Later, we decided to do this together as a couple. I wanted to have a place — a home — and be settled in it and ready for kids to come into it before getting pregnant.

Catherine: We were in this group of friends who would have dinner parties and everyone would talk about how they would have kids, how they wanted to do it and all the different issues. I think it was such an incredible experience because all of the couples were interracial and some have had their kids already and some are still planning it.

We went to the Michigan Womyn's Music Festival one year and attended a "Women in Interracial Relationships" workshop. There was a couple with a little girl there and they felt really alienated and isolated in their community and didn't know any other "mixed" couples. We said we didn't know many other couples who weren't "mixed." To have that community and have a place where you can share ideas and support is pretty amazing. In other parts of the country and various parts of the community, people don't have any kind of support.

Melanie: When we were getting ready to have Sadie Rain, Catherine was sort of "iffy" about wanting to be pregnant. I was sure I wanted to be pregnant, so I went first.

Catherine: We knew we wanted a known donor. We wanted Sadie to know her biological father. We also wanted someone we knew, so we'd know his personality, his intelligence, temperament, biology and health. We have a lot of extended family, both in our biological families and among our friends, and he's a part of that. He's an artist and lives nearby.

Melanie: My family's in New Jersey and Catherine's are in uptown Manhattan. They dash over for lunch sometimes. It's really nice that we've always had a lot of support from our families. It's always been very inclusive.

Catherine: I'm in the process of adopting Sadie. In New York state, you can do second-parent, same-gender adoptions. It will help with schools and medical issues and there will never be a legal question that I'm her parent. The other nice thing is that she has both of our last names, which has already made a difference when traveling. At the airport, they'll say, "Sadie Rain Hope Saalfield. She has both of your names!" I can sign anything and they don't ask to see proof that I'm her parent.

Melanie: Because of the way Sadie looks, a lot of times, people don't know which one of us was pregnant with her.

> **"I'm in the process of adopting Sadie. It will help with schools and medical issues and there will never be a legal question that I'm her parent."**

Catherine: People ask me all the time how I lost all that weight so fast.

Melanie: And if she's breast-feeding.

Catherine: I'm doing primary child-care now, so I spend a lot of time with her in the day and out in the world. People come up all the time and say, "She's so cute. She looks just like you." It's so funny.

Melanie: She *does* look like you.

Catherine: Actually, in the beginning, I used to explain the whole thing, I'd get so anxious. And then I stopped. I wanted to allow myself to just be her mother without always having to explain it. Instead I just say, "thank you" or whatever. I want to encourage their instinctive recognition that they saw me with my beautiful daughter. They don't need to know the whole story.

Melanie: Even though a lot of lesbians and gay men are having kids in our generation, it's still sort of a big deal. When I was pregnant, people didn't know I was a lesbian when I was by myself. When we're together, it really throws people off. They try to figure out what's going on and whose kid it is. They ask us both that. I think some of them probably don't think it's ours at all. They think we're just watching somebody else's kid.

Catherine: I took Sadie to her doctor's appointment one day. She said, "Oh, well, are you the designated mom today?" I said, "No, I'm her mom everyday." The doctor said, "This must be fun for you to take her to her doctor's appointment." And I'm thinking, "No, not at all." She's trying to say the right thing, but she's acting like I'm her aunt and I'm taking care of her for the afternoon — which is what aunts do.

On the day Sadie Rain was born, *Newsweek* magazine hit the stands with Melissa Etheridge and Julie Cypher on the cover. And it said, "We're Having A Baby." People sent us that magazine and some people left messages about it. I think it was a point of reference for a much more mainstream society. They see two women can have a kid. Actually, when Melanie got back from the hospital, she wanted to have ten more kids. She was delirious.

Melanie: It was so exciting. The birth was such a high. You forget about the hard part.

Catherine: Anywhere we go, we're going to take her. She's going to come with us and see the world. She'll teach us things in a way that we might not see otherwise. On her first trip we took her to the island where her great-grandparents are from. But we couldn't lie on the beach or sleep late. She definitely made us see it differently. With her, we walked all over that island every day. I feel like she's a partner with us. She'll help us know what she needs and how she wants to be.

Melanie: A lot of that is going to be revealed. We're both very dedicated to letting her be who she truly is.

> **Anywhere we go, we're going to take her. She's going to come with us and see the world. She'll teach us things in a way that we might not see otherwise.**

" All of a sudden, one day, I said, 'I don't want to be with men anymore.' My friends said, 'You must be depressed.' I said, 'No, I think I'm a lesbian.' "

Ramona Gonzales calls herself a "hair-healer" or a "hairdresser-from-hell." She has soft red hair, green eyes and wears orange lipstick. She shares her life with her partner Joanne Avila, who works for a theatre box office, their 10-year-old daughter Maximillian, whom she calls "mija," and their cat, "Chile." Maximillian likes ghost stories, reads at least one book a day, has maps of the U.S. and the world on her bedroom wall and was named after her grandmother's brother. As we sat in their living room together, hip hop music played softly in the kitchen. Max told us that it was "her fault" that her mother eventually met and fell in love with Joanne. And Joanne knew, in spite of shyness and a few obstacles, that she had finally met her true love.

Ramona: I was born Ramona Elizabeth Gonzales in 1952 in San Francisco. I'm third-generation Mexican-American and was raised Catholic.

Joanne: I am Joanne Marie Avila, born in 1959 in San Jose, California. I'm also third-generation Mexican-American and was raised Catholic.

Ramona: By the time I was 21, I went to Oregon and was living with a bunch of hippies in a commune, raising goats and doing that whole Oregon hippie thing. All of a sudden, one day, I said, "I don't want to be with men anymore. This is just not a challenge to me emotionally and spiritually." My friends said, "You must be depressed." I said "No, I think I'm a lesbian." Then, I went to Seattle and I officially came out in 1977, and the dykes hated me because I wore dresses and make-up. That was just not the "heavy, revy, leftist lezzy's" way. I thought they were very oppressive women and decided to live my lesbian life the way I wanted to.

Joanne: I knew I was gay when I was little. I'd say when I was four, I was pretty much aware that I liked women or girls and by the time I was in second grade, I was totally in love with my teacher who was a nun.

Ramona: When Max was about three, she and I were at a burger joint called "Hot 'N Hunky's." She was dancing to the juke box when she saw Joanne and her roommate Sam. Joanne had a flat top, but Max knew she was a girl. Max said, "Do you think that woman would dance with me if I asked her?" Then she got really shy, so I said, "My daughter wants to dance with you."

Joanne: I said, "Well, she has good taste," and thought, "I know I'm going to marry this woman." So when they finished eating and got up to leave, sure enough, Ramona turned around and looked at me and smiled. About six months later, we met at Cafe Flor and Ramona asked me to come to her house. I saw the Micky Mouse table sitting in a corner and thought to myself, "If I'm getting involved with this woman, who has a child, am I committed enough?" We've been together ever since. It was in that split second in the living room that our family came together.

All my thought processes were focused on the foundation I needed to create for this little girl to trust me and make sure she's very happy in her life. Part of that was being sober for 13 years.

Ramona: Max really makes sure you're an okay person before she welcomes you into her realm. She was cautious for about six months. She would come between us physically when we would hug in the beginning. She wouldn't let Joanne carry her.

The community can be really oppressive if you don't fit the mold. At school, I feel like there's this hidden pressure to succeed as mothers and prove to everybody out there that not only are we *good* mothers, but possibly better because there's two of us. We haven't always been welcomed as lesbian mothers even within the gay community because if you're not artificially inseminated or you didn't adopt your child ... you're a parent, but you're not really an "official lesbian mother" if you had your baby from a heterosexual union.

Before Joanne and I got together, Max and I had a really rough time for about five months. We didn't have any money and we were walking down the Castro when a woman was soliciting donations for their women's softball league. I couldn't afford to buy a raffle ticket and she said, "It's a dollar" and I said, "I don't have a dollar." "Well, excuse my language," she said, "Get your straight ass and your straight kid out of our neighborhood." I thought, "Do I need a sign that says 'lesbian mother' because I don't fit your mold?"

Joanne: I work with a lot of straight people who are much more open.

Ramona: Max always marches with us in the Gay Pride parade. The year we won our custody battle — which was a horrific thing to go through — we were so happy to be there. But the moms just looked at us. The gay dads were the nicest ones to us. That was hard.

I was 34 when Max was born. Her father was 22. We weren't married and we weren't a couple. I just knew this guy through friends at the modeling agency where I worked. It was a one-night stand. The one and only time I slept with him I used a diaphragm and I knew in less than a week that I was pregnant. After Max was born, we foolishly married. He's twelve years younger than I am, so the level of responsibility was a huge frustration.

In the custody dispute, we felt no support from the lesbian community or our friends. Our search for a lawyer was exhausting and it came down to money. We began to fear it was because we were Latinas. My lesbianism became a focus of the custody issues and along with that came a question of my ability to mother and parent Max.

In this custody battle, many horrible things were said about me, my lifestyle and who I was as a mother to my daughter. Every day we work to put that all behind us, but the threat remains and that scares the hell out of me.

> "The community can be really oppressive if you don't fit the mold. At school, I feel like there's this hidden pressure to succeed as mothers and prove to everybody out there that not only are we good mothers, but possibly better because there's two of us."

MURIEL MIGUEL WITH HER DAUGHTER MURIELLE AND GRANDDAUGHTER JOSEPHINE
New York

uriel Miguel lives in an old, three-story house in Brooklyn with Debra, her partner of eight years. As we come up a dark stairwell, a statue of Minnehaha sits in a niche in the hallway. Old pictures, beads and rattles cover the mantel along with baby pictures of her granddaughter Josephine. Muriel has two grown daughters, Murielle (28) and Calle (25), and one granddaughter, age three. Muriel is also an actress, director, playwright, teacher and elder. She is a mesmerizing storyteller, one of the *grande dames* of Spiderwoman Theatre, the oldest continually running women's theatre company in North America, which she founded in 1976 with her sisters.

I was born in 1937 in Brooklyn, of a Kuna father and a Rappahannock mother. My father and mother met in this house. My father comes from a tribe that's off the coast of Panama, on the San Blas Islands, and they live the same way they lived centuries ago. They are great seamen. My father was a merchant marine and he docked here in Brooklyn.

My grandmother was a midwife and an herbalist. So we were all born on the floor here. My grandmother delivered all of us. My mother was really treated differently because she was born with a caul — it's a piece of extra skin. It's the sign, when you're born, that you're psychic. Josey, my granddaughter was born with a second skin also.

It was hard growing up. My father was a drunk and you're very noticeable if you're an Indian family. You're certainly not Italian. You look different and you do different things. You wear your hair long. And my mother was a psychic, which was not a happy thing for me. The idea that my mother could read tea leaves was awful for me. She was called *strega* — "witch" — on the block. These women didn't mind having their tea leaves read, but they also called her a witch and they made fun of us. My father was called "Wahoo" and "Tonto."

I was a tough little street kid. What saved me was my culture. We lived amongst other Indian families — Mohawk steelworkers who came straight down from Montreal into Brooklyn. I grew up with a Hopi/Winnebago family next door. We grew up with all these other people who brought their living cultures here to the city. That's what saved me. I was never ashamed of being Indian.

I call myself Two-Spirit. I have an Indian name that was given to me a couple of years ago. It means "third daughter from the stars." It's the family name from the Kuna and it's a creation story. The second half of my name means "twins." Isn't that amazing? I wish I had known it earlier.

The year before my first daughter was born, my father died. I knew at the funeral that the next year I was going to have a child. I found an Indian man because I knew I wanted Indian children and married him. He was much younger than me and I had my first child, Murielle.

I remember that I took all these natural childbirth classes and of course my husband didn't want to come. I did this all by myself. I was determined that I was going to see everything, so I wouldn't take any drugs. I was at Roosevelt Hospital here in New York City and it was the beginning of the midwifery R.N. program, so I had a midwife who was wonderful.

They whisked me in and of course I didn't see anything. My eyes were shut. The terrible thing I remember was, after the afterbirth, this guy started to stitch me up and I wanted to leave. But the episiotomy had to be stitched up. He was taking so long.

" This is my life. This is my sexual preference. It is not an alternative. The other part was the experimentation and I finally got down to what was good. "

"Well, it was like they dropped off the edge of the world. He took them and I couldn't get to them. Those were very awful, dark days for six years. "

Finally, I sat up and said, "What are you doing? Are you making a flag? Come on!" (Laughs).

Then with my other daughter Calle, we had gone to the movies to see Marlon Brando. We were very poor and in the lobby on 42nd Street my water broke, but we had spent a lot of money to see this movie, so I sat there. I have no idea how the movie ended. All I remember is Marlon Brando. I finally called up the hospital and they said, "Take a taxi!"

When Murielle was eight or nine, she got an acting job on one of these serials on PBS called "Vegetable Soup." She was the youngest one with all these smart showbiz kids. She worked very hard on four or five episodes. When she finally got her check, we took the money and went to buy her school clothing. I was bringing up little frilly dresses and matching things and everything she brought to me, I'd say "no." Finally she brought this blue suit with white pants and I said, "No, that's going to get dirty." She got very angry and said, "Listen, this is my money. I worked very hard for this money and I think I have a right to choose my clothes." Well, she was right. I realized at that moment that my child was developing her own style and making her own choices.

At the time I was working in theatre and was going to Europe, but my mother couldn't take care of the kids, so they went with my husband. He asked me if it was all right to take the kids to Colorado. I said "Yes," as long as I was able to be in contact with them and take them when I got back. Well, it was like they dropped off the edge of the world. He took them and I couldn't get to them. He told his family

not to tell me where they were. Then the kids turned and said they didn't want to see me. Those were very awful, dark days for six years.

When Murielle turned 18, I got a message from a friend of mine, an ex-sister-in-law. She said "I'm not supposed to do this, but I'm giving you the phone number of where Murielle is staying. Happy Mother's Day!" Mother's Day always hit me hard because I didn't have my kids. Murielle got on the phone and said "Hello" and started to talk to me like she saw me yesterday.

My greatest challenge was keeping my kids. Even now I fill up because it was so devastating. I would remember them as babies, and now they were teenagers and I had no say at all. When I did get them back, my girlfriend at the time said I would have to choose between them and her. Anyone who makes you choose that is awful! I had just gotten them back.

Your responsibility as a gay parent is to raise healthy kids because people assume you won't. So you raise them and it's done. You've done your thing. No matter what they do, you're finished. A lot of dykes are raising boys now. It's wonderful. It teaches a lot — a whole new perspective to a whole new generation. And then, it's not just your responsibility. It moves on to another generation.

Somehow, I don't think marriage is the solution to homophobia — this whole thing about gays getting married and being like other people. What runs through my mind about homophobia is, "This is not an alternative for me. This is my life. This is my sexual preference. It is not an alternative. The other part was the experimentation and I finally got down to what was good."

> **All of a sudden I wasn't given the respect that my rank earned me, I was in a relationship that was about to end, and I was out in the middle of the Indian Ocean.**

Cindy Acker and "Milly" Jessen live in a blue Victorian on a wide boulevard lined with big trees. Born in 1956 in San Francisco, Cindy is of African and Native American descent and is an administrator and teacher for a Montessori school. Born in New York City in 1951, Milly is Puerto Rican, was raised in Spanish Harlem and is a teacher. They have four children, Jennifer (16), Brionna (13), Jonathan (11) and Eric (8), a black cat named "Night" and a bull python called "Tod." Often finishing each other's sentences and holding hands during their interview, they invited us to stay for dinner.

Cindy: I was a very sheltered Jehovah's Witness teenager and young person. I had no idea what a lesbian was. I knew that I had some different feelings. I knew there was something called homosexuality and that it was wrong.

Milly: I realized at the age of five that I was different. I had my first relationship when I was 13. I came out to my parents when I was 18. After that, I didn't talk to them for a very long time.

Cindy: As a Jehovah's Witness, I never watched television or saw movies I shouldn't watch. I never read any books that weren't Jehovah's Witness books. I became what's called a "pioneer," someone who goes door-to-door 100 hours a month. I eventually went to a therapist and said, "Whenever I walk down the street, every woman that I see I'm wondering about her: how soft she is, what it would be like to go to coffee with her or what her house looks like."

Milly: I spent 12 years in the Navy and was very closeted at the time. I was a chief of middle management and an excellent sailor. The day I turned myself in as a lesbian, I became the worst thing in the world. All of a sudden I wasn't given the respect that my rank earned me, I was in a relationship that was about to end, and I was out in the middle of the Indian Ocean.

Cindy: I got married when I was 17 and I talked to my husband about everything I felt. His answer was that I needed to read the Bible more and go to services. Finally I moved out of the bedroom. We lived in a gorgeous five-level house filled with beautiful antique furniture. I moved down to the lower level next to the garage and slept on the floor for three years.

I had been completely dependent on my husband financially. One day while he was gone at work, I left and took what was in the children's bedrooms. I left everything else. I took a bag of clothes and some underwear. Then I found this house. I made a deal with the landlord with no money and she said, "Okay."

I wondered if this was the best thing for my children. But I knew that the situation I was in with my husband was not an honest one. If I didn't give my children anything else, I knew I needed to be honest about who I was and they needed to understand the importance of that.

Milly: About that time, I met Cindy at a conference on Children with AIDS in 1988. I fell in love with her. She was very eloquent. We had a short meeting, "Hi. Hello." That's it.

Cindy: I ran back up to my hotel room and changed into this black leather-looking pantsuit because I thought it looked "lesbian-ish." I thought this must be what a lesbian looked like. I came back down to the lobby and everyone had already left.

Milly: I was still living with my ex at the time, although our relationship had technically ended. I worked all day and came home and took care of our son Eric who we had adopted at birth. He was premature, 10 weeks early. He weighed 3 lbs., 4 oz. at birth. He was in the preemie nursery for six weeks and then came to our house. He became "my little guy." We put everything into Eric, lived in the same house, but I lived upstairs with Eric. It was an interesting sphere — two bubbles that never quite met. So I decided to leave.

Cindy: One night Milly was over and I sang Barbra Streisand in the kitchen. She was standing against the wall and she started to slide down onto the floor.

Milly: I had it real bad. By then, I realized I was totally in love with Cindy. I felt like a teenager all over again. I told her everything she ever wanted or needed was right in this little package here — me. And she said, "No, it ain't gonna happen."

Cindy: I was still sorting out feelings. She was for the first time seeing things for herself and baring those things in front of me and hoping to god that I wasn't going to take advantage of that. On May 23, 1993, she said, "I have exposed my heart and come to know myself at the same time. And I know if this doesn't work, I'll be okay." I wrote that in my journal because that freed me to love her and to make a commitment.

Milly: Yep. That's basically it. Of course we had the merging of families. I only have Eric part-time. I share custody with my ex and I pay child support.

Cindy: Jennifer said to me one day, "Couldn't you find someone else? Why did it have to be Milly?" I said,

"What is it about Milly that you don't like?" She said, "I love Milly. But why couldn't it be a man?" And I said, "Because then it wouldn't be Milly." She was silent and then said, "That makes sense. Got it."

Brionna's question was, "Why in the world didn't you leave the marriage a whole lot earlier? It would have been nice if you would have been clearer with me." And Jonathan had a heck of a time. He still does. When Milly moved in, she opened a door for him. She came in real butchy. I took Jonathan out to tea. We went to antique shops. One day he was acting up when we went out to tea. When I asked him why, he said, "Because I want to play basketball." So Milly came in with bats and balls.

Milly: I was a catcher in the Navy. I was very athletic and played second base all summer.

Cindy: So Jonathan and Milly really connected because of that. In terms of parenting, it's a whole lot safer for the kids to talk to us because there's an intensity and closeness that's not just inherent to having a good relationship, but also comes from the fact that we're lesbians.

They say the hardest part about having lesbian mothers is that we're very in sync and we're very consistent. They can't play off us as much. They say, "You always feel the same way she does." Even though we may have different opinions, they know there is a consistent bottom line.

Our family stands out without saying anything. Wherever we go, our family makes an incredible statement because of who we are.

> " In terms of parenting, it's a whole lot safer for the kids to talk to us because there's an intensity and closeness that's not just inherent to having a good relationship, but also comes from the fact that we're lesbians. "

Kuʻumeaaloha Gomes is a leading activist for Native Hawaiʻian sovereignty rights, Director of Recruitment at the University of Hawaiʻi, Honolulu, and is working on her Ph.D. in political science. She and her 31-year-old son Lawrence met us at *Hanaiakamalama,* now known as Queen Emma's Summer Palace in Nuuanu Valley. They sat on the grass amidst mango and tamarind trees, reminiscing together while Kuʻumeaaloha's partner, Kalai, sat nearby. While offering us *poi, lomi, laulua* and raw fish for lunch, Kuʻumeaaloha spoke passionately of her love for her son, the land and *Kanaka Maoli* — her native Hawaiʻian people.

In our culture, the grandmother or great aunt names the child. I was born on May 10, 1945, and my grandmother had a dream the night before I was born. My father called her to tell of my birth and the first thing she said was, "Her name will be Kuʻumeaaloha," which means "the place that love comes from."

I have to live my name because in our culture, it is believed when you don't live your name, your spirit will die. "Ha" means "breathe of life" and it is also the taro plant which is our staple food. When we say, "Aloha," we're actually saying, "I share my breath of life with you so that you continue to live."

At a very young age, I learned about inclusion and struggle and the need for people to feel nurtured. My grandmother used to share a story with me about *pau a pau* and *Makuahine* or Earth Mother and her children. It was so soothing to understand the perpetual nurturance and acceptance of my life. This earth is centuries old but she is the greatest role model. A mother doesn't throw her children away, she thinks of what's best for them. I've learned a lot of lessons just by looking at our Earth Mother and how she does things.

Those stories continue to influence me as a gay woman. Whether we're American Indian, Hawaiʻian, women who are poor, affluent, married or divorced, as a community, we're working together to overcome oppression. That should be the key that opens all doors.

I think political education at a very young age is important for children — to talk about equality and diversity and reveal the contradictions in society. If our children learn this early on, they can make good decisions and avoid discriminating against others and themselves.

I was married four times to two different men, but it was never because of my passion or love for them. I wanted acceptance from my father and stepmother. I would be with men, but when we'd be making love, I'd be fantasizing about making love to a woman. Because I came from a strong, conservative Catholic family, being gay was not something I knew about. It was never my world.

When I married Lawrence's father, he was my first and only boyfriend in high school. I was pregnant when I married him. I was 20 years old and I enjoyed the pregnancy because I felt I had a miracle growing inside of me. In a lot of ways, his father didn't matter. I was in love with my baby. I thought Lawrence was the most beautiful baby. I raised him almost by myself. I was a single parent working full-time. We had a very hard time financially, so he's not spoiled and we made a little go a long way.

I remember how difficult it was to be a woman raising a son and not be able to be a coach on a basketball team or a baseball team because it was all men. A place where a woman could be involved in was in Cub

> **I have to live my name because in our culture, it is believed when you don't live your name, your spirit will die.**

> **I was 20 years old and I enjoyed the pregnancy because I felt I had a miracle growing inside of me. In a lot of ways, his father didn't matter. I was in love with my baby.**

Scouts as a den mother. That was real boring to me, so I was on the periphery.

I tried to instill certain values in Lawrence that were not religious values, but basically moral values. Getting along with people and knowing right from wrong. We had special times together. We were each other's friends. He did so many things that were precious as a child. One time, when he was four years old, I was serving broccoli for dinner for the first time. We were having fried chicken with gravy, rice and broccoli with butter. When I set out his plate for him, he was just looking at it and tears started coming down. I said, "Lawrence, are you okay?" He said, "Mom, why are you making me eat little trees?"

Now, when we're together, we sing. We do karaoke at his house. We have some favorite songs by the Carpenters that I can sing. He has a beautiful voice and he'll say, "Mom, this one is for you!" It's really neat. He's quite the comedian and he enjoys seeing me laugh. We can also sit down and talk politics, and he can give me feedback on issues I'm involved with.

My greatest challenge as a mother was the struggle to just be open and to accept who I was and then to

know how to adjust to that in society. Lawrence never knew what it was like for me to struggle as a gay woman. When he was 16, he decided to go live with his dad. That's when I decided to go live with a woman.

In my thirties, I started hanging out with Hawai'ian women, and that was the beginning of my "coming out" process. By this time, I was immersed in the Hawai'ian land rights struggle and went to New Zealand as an international guest for the Maori land struggles movement.

This group of women were called the "Maori dykes" and we traveled from city to city doing community organizing. Every night I watched these women take care of each other. They massaged each other and told stories and braided each other's hair. They were not necessarily lovers, but I saw the intimacy and intensity of their love. I never had experienced anything like that. I began to feel overwhelmed with love and respect for these women. Something was opening up for me and coming through for the first time, gushing with passion. Then I knew I wanted to be with women.

GAYLE BRICKERT-ALBRECHT AND RENATÉ FEARONCE WITH GRIFFIN AND DASHIELL

Arizona

Gayle Brickert-Albrecht and Renaté Fearonce live with their two sons, Griffin (10) and Dashiell (7), two rabbits, "Rosie" the rat, dog "Chloe," four turtles and two cats, "Rajah" and "Philatelic." Gayle is a 41-year-old high school chemistry teacher born in Chehalis, Washington, and Renaté is a 41-year-old post office clerk born in Nuremberg, Germany. They each gave birth through an anonymous donor insemination and have joint legal custody of their sons. On the Sunday morning we arrived, Dashiell had just returned from soccer practice in a black, white and red striped uniform and Griffin was playing in the driveway.

Renaté: The joys of being a mother are the little things you see. Like when people tell me what manners Griffin and Dashiell have and how well-behaved they are, outside our home.

Gayle: My favorite moments are when the boys enjoy each other's company and are getting along. They can get into a creative play situation where they've got a little police station going in the living room or a fort in the back up in a tree. They bicker a little, but on the grand scale of things, they don't fight very much.

Renaté: Raising them with positive values is a big challenge these days with all the negative stuff that's out there in the world. It's really hard to shield them from it and explain it all to them and equip them to deal with it as adults.

Gayle: Since I teach, I see a lot of kids who have a lot of material things and stuff around them, but they don't feel secure and safe. They don't feel loved in their families.

On the other hand, both Griffin and Dashiell don't necessarily have a strong perception of what a family "should" be like. They've never watched Leave It To Beaver. One night, we had an old friend babysitting them and she was talking about when she was growing up and her parents divorced. Dashiell said, "Oh, did you come from a family that has two moms or two dads or one of each?" As if they were all logical choices. He doesn't see any differences.

Renaté: Our family was profiled in the paper here two years ago. The title ran, *"Two Moms: That's the Way It Is"* because when the reporter asked Griffin about his mothers, he said, "I have two moms. That's the way it is." After the article came out, I realized how freeing that was and how much support we had from people all over the place.

Gayle: Even people we hardly knew would come up to us and thank us for doing the story. For some people, it made a huge difference just to see our family out there.

Renaté: People see that we have the same values as other families. We nurture our children. We spend most of our time driving our kids to soccer practice and trying to keep the house straightened up. Our boys are happy, confident, proud and feel good about themselves. That's the way it is.

Debra Olson lives in Tarzana with her daughters Chrysta (13) and Kaitlyn (8), "Denmark" the dalmatian, three African tortoises, "Macho," "Picchu" and "Taos," two rabbits, "Holly" and "Honey," and two cats, "Little Owl" and "Sweetie Pie." Debra was born in 1949 and raised in Beverly Hills, graduating magna cum laude from UCLA with a degree in political science and business. Her grandfather, Culbert L. Olson, was the first Democratic governor of California. Her grandmother, Elijah King Olson, was an early suffragette leader in the U.S. Presently a board member of President Clinton's Democratic Leadership Council, which formulates policy for the Democratic Party, Debra is also Chief Consultant and the Founding Distributor for FutureNet Online, Inc., a high tech and utility marketing company.

I always knew I wanted to be a mother. Through the years, I dated men and attempted to be straight, although I knew when I was 13 that I preferred girls. I had a boyfriend in high school and we went steady for a couple years. Later, I left him for a woman, which broke his heart. When I was 17, I became a Buddhist, practiced celibacy and lived in Japan. During my late twenties, I traveled the globe for two years, studying with the Maharishi in India, climbing the Himalayas and living near the Great Pyramids of Egypt, sleeping on the arm of The Giant Sphinx. I was into women, but my focus was developing spiritually.

In 1981, it was the beginning of the insemination movement that's now emerged for many women having children. I really wanted to have children and every guy I looked at was viewed as a potential donor. I asked two of my Hollywood buddies, John Travolta and Warren Beatty, and they said, "Thanks for thinking of me, but no thanks." They both wanted to be active dads. After a serious meditation on finding a donor, I went to my beauty salon in Beverly Hills one day and saw this young man getting his hair cut. The minute I saw him, I knew he was perfect. So I asked him to lunch, explained my situation, and offered him a four-figure sum of money. He was a New Age kind of guy, intelligent, gorgeous and spiritual. He said, "Yes!"

We became friends and decided to do it at my house — not make love, but inseminate. We lit candles and did a meditation and I conceived Chrysta then. It was a conscious conception with two individuals who were not into making love with each other, but were friends. I'm glad I did it that way. Chrysta was born October 22, 1984. It was a great celebration.

Chrysta wanted a sister, so four and a half years later, we did the same kind of meditation and insemination and Kaitlyn was conceived. Kaitlyn was born on March 19, 1989. It's been an unbelievable experience. In retrospect I wouldn't have done anything differently. Through the years their father, the girls, and I have developed a very strong union.

I have been blessed with two precious daughters. I have loved the whole experience of raising them: birthing, breastfeeding, the first day of kindergarten, the challenge of getting them into the best schools that give

> **During my late twenties, I traveled the globe for two years, studying with the Maharishi in India, climbing the Himalayas and living near the Great Pyramids of Egypt, sleeping on the arm of The Giant Sphinx.**

" The minute I saw

him, I knew he was

perfect. So I asked him

to lunch, explained my

situation, and offered

him a four-figure sum

of money. **"**

them quality education. Both of my kids are incredible human beings. They're both artistic and incredibly open and beautiful. At 13, Chrysta wants to be a designer, and she prefers old black and white movies from the 30s and 40s. Both of them are staunch vegetarians and they don't hesitate to share their feelings about hurting animals with other people. They're both straight-A students. Not that they have to be perfect, but they're functioning at a really healthy level.

You have to be ready for motherhood. It's an exhausting job is what I say to all my friends whose clocks are ticking. I have to get up at 5:30 every morning and make their lunches and drive them to school. I just recently set up a college fund for both of them. It's hard to do it alone. There's no more sleeping until 10 in the morning or having wild romantic love affairs. It has been challenging to not have a lifetime partner. I would like to find a truly compatible lover to share the rest of my life with.

My other challenges are financial. My entire life I've always had courage, but to have the guts to raise two kids on your own is a big deal. There have been points when I've made $200,000 a year and times when I haven't made a dime. I've been through tremendous financial trauma, but I've always trusted the universe. Right now, I'm making an excellent living, but a year ago, I wasn't. It was good for my kids to see what it was like to not have money. I see kids who are raised with so much affluence, they absolutely don't have the value of knowing what it's like to struggle and make it.

Giving my daughters a spiritual base and honesty is very important. I've always been an open lesbian. I've always talked about my feelings. A big responsibility is also giving them exposure to individuals who have achieved greatness. For instance, I've taken them to lectures by Maya Angelou. I always try to expose them to extraordinary poets, artists, revolutionaries, actors, educators and visionaries.

Every day I get up at sunrise and I wake up my girls for school and sing "It's a Beautiful Day in the Neighborhood," the Mr. Rogers song. I just go and kiss them. They've both probably had a million kisses. Just kissing them and hugging them and loving them every day is what I cherish.

Justina Trott is an M.D. and director of women's health services at a city hospital. Nedra DiFilippo, her partner of five years, and their eight-year-old daughter Ari live in a comfortable, old adobe house with a 1956 turquoise and cream-colored Chevy parked in the driveway. Possessing an earthy radiance and warmth, Justina is half-Sicilian and half-Neapolitan. Nedra is also Italian-American, has short salt-and-pepper hair, is a visual artist and is Ari's non-biological parent. As we all sat together at a round oak table in the dining room sipping tea, two Abyssinian cats wandered around the room. While we spoke, Ari's grandmother, visiting from Michigan, popped her head in from the kitchen periodically.

Justina: I was born in Connecticut in 1948 in the Stratford-Bridgeport area. I was born into a traditional Italian-Catholic family that was pretty extended. We lived in a neighborhood where my aunts, uncles, cousins and my grandparents all lived within three or four blocks of one another.

I never thought about whether I'd get married or not but I just assumed I'd have many children. I was raised Catholic-Italian, right? So I thought I'd have about seven kids. Then when I became involved with a woman when I was 22 and had all these career plans, it was something I didn't think about for many years.

Around 1982, I started feeling like I really wanted to get serious about having a child. I talked to some friends about whether they would be interested in donating sperm. I went to the state law library and did some reading on custody issues. Finally I decided on alternative insemination. I got information from the sperm bank and again looked at the legal and custody issues and medical issues as well, because at that time — it was the early eighties and HIV-testing wasn't routine.

I was not with a partner at that point. I was alone and I just decided then that I was going to get pregnant and I did. I decided that it would be just fine to do it on my own.

One of the funniest things I remember was one of the physicians at the hospital where I work, who is maybe in his sixties, said to one of the physicians in the emergency room, "Well, how could she be pregnant and have a baby? I mean, she's not married!"

My parents did not come to visit me during the time period when I was pregnant. Actually the first time that they actually came to visit was on Ari's first birthday. They really couldn't handle it very well. But after they met Ari, things have been fine. My mother's birthday is the day before Ari's, so they come and spend their birthdays together.

Nedra: When Justina and I first started to develop a relationship, I remember Ari was real little and she looked up at me and said, "What are you doing here again? You're not part of this family!" Part of that was just the psychological reality that their connection for three-and-a-half years was with no one else around and their relationship was being intruded upon.

Now Ari knows about sex, love, friendship and commitment. But for a long time, Ari was just coming to an understanding of what our relationship was — the sexual and emotional component and the commitment.

One day she said, "You can't do it. You have to have a bride and a groom on top of the wedding cake and that is it." I said, "Where did you ever see a wedding cake with the bride and groom?" And she said, "On t.v." So those messages are subtle and powerful.

Another time, when we first got involved and were traveling in Italy together, Ari told somebody on the plane that I was her mother's lover — probably while this man was quietly eating his peanuts. We really did well and didn't panic. We let her psyche evolve the way she needed it to evolve.

As a caretaker of Ari, subtle stuff comes up with other children. Children can be so much more conservative in their views about what the world looks like. When they see another female adult who has an intimate relationship with Ari, they look very subtly and they're figuring it out or questioning or maybe they think

it's weird. I don't think that's discrimination, it's simply how children operate when they're confronted with something different.

When Ari was four, I went for a parent-teacher meeting and there was a list of mothers and fathers and what they did. Ari had me in the father slot. Her teacher told me she wanted me in there — not as a father, but she had me in the father slot as an artist.

Justina: Our roles are pretty fluid. There are ways in which Nedra can be with Ari that I can't be and vice versa.

Nedra: I've been fortunate that Justina has never imposed her philosophy or feelings on what goes on between Ari and me. We talk about problems and I make my own mistakes. I marvel at that.

Justina: I was older; I was 37 when I had Ari. I had a lot of years to go through my own individuation. Meeting Nedra and knowing a lot about ourselves on an emotional level helped enormously. Ari has parents who are self-defined.

There's this old saying and I don't know where it comes from, that it takes a whole village to raise a child. There's no question in my mind that it's absolutely true. I think the more a child is exposed to, in terms of skills, teaching and approaches to life, obviously the better off the child is.

KAREN GOETZ AND MARY ALICE BALL WITH LAURA
Arizona

Karen Goetz and Mary Alice Ball sat around the dining room table for their interview with their three-year-old strawberry-blonde daughter Laura beside them. Karen is a 44-year-old health care professional from San Francisco whose "great-great-grand-mother crossed the plains to California in a covered wagon." Mary Alice is a 44-year-old doctoral candidate from New Jersey, working on her Ph.D. in higher education technology policy. They met 10 years ago in Chicago at a theatre performance.

Mary Alice: I put off trying to have a child for years, thinking I could do it anytime. When I was 38, I tried to get pregnant for two years and was unsuccessful. That was a really painful time. I rode an emotional roller coaster with each insemination and ultimate disappointment. Eventually I just decided to give up and concentrate on graduate school.

Karen: I started out much less enthusiastic about having children and I went through my own process during those two years. I did some private envisioning of us as a family and pictured a baby with us. Gradually I found myself very invested in the idea and by the time Mary Alice said, "Forget it!" I was saying, "We have to find a way to be a family." We took a break and then I started taking my temperature and charting my cycle.

Mary Alice: Eventually Karen tried to get pregnant with a donation from the same donor I had used and got pregnant on the first try.

Karen: Mary Alice was accepted into the doctoral program the same week I became pregnant!

Mary Alice: So I decided to defer my fellowship for a year. We had Laura in Chicago and then moved when she was seven months old. Because Laura was born in Cook County, it turned out I was able to legally adopt her. Just three days before we moved, the adoption judgment was final — that was July 28, 1995. It was definitely, without question, the greatest joy I've had since her birth. We were grateful for the other couples — the pioneers — who led the way.

Karen: For me, the adoption meant that Mary Alice's dream had finally come true. We were legitimate in the eyes of the law in this country and the integrity of our family could not be challenged. Laura represents a whole series of decisions about truth for me. My greatest joy is knowing that I am living a life of truth, that I've created a family of my dreams. I made no compromises. I didn't give in to anybody else's image of me. I didn't give in to my own fears or discomfort with who I am or what I want.

I've always believed that Laura truly is a product of us both because Mary Alice gave birth to the idea and I gave birth to the child. The other part of the magic is the moment she was born — 12:05 a.m. on Christmas morning. When she was born, the doctor said, "She's reaching for the sky!" Laura stretched her little arms up as they were lifting her out and Mary Alice and I wept, we were so excited. This image of this precious little being coming into the world, not in fear, but reaching upward and out, will stay in my mind forever. That is the way I want to live.

"For me, the adoption meant that Mary Alice's dream had finally come true. We were legitimate in the eyes of the law in this country and the integrity of our family could not be challenged."

SHARON DAY WITH HER DAUGHTERS SUZIE AND MELISSA, GRANDCHILDREN JOEY, DEON AND KIRBY, SISTER DORENE, BROTHER MICHAEL AND NIECES/NEPHEWS ARIANA, JAMES, ALYSSA, ALANA AND CHARLOTTE

Minnesota

Sharon Day is Executive Director for the Minnesota American Indian AIDS Task Force. We met her family in St. Paul, where everyone gathered in a courtyard outside her apartment building. Wearing a ribbon shirt and glasses, Sharon sat in the center with her daughters Suzie (27) and Melissa (25) by her side. Her three grandchildren, Joey (2), Deon (6) — and Kirby (8) whom Sharon has legal custody of and who she has raised since birth — gathered around her. Her sister Dorene and her five children, Ariana (17), James (15), Alyssa (10), Alana (7) and Charlotte (1), joined her. Sharon said, "Dorene is nine years younger than me. I got to be a second mother to her. Her children and I are very close and we see each other almost every day." Also present is Sharon's brother, Michael, wearing the baseball cap.

We call ourselves *Aninishabe*. A lot of people call us Ojibewe. Both of my parents are from the same reservation in northern Minnesota and most of us were born there.

I have a ceremonial name, *Nagahmoo Mahengin*, which translates into "Singing Wolf." When I think about my name, it gives me something to aspire to — to take care of the young, to care for the elderly, to be a social creature. I'm not a very good social creature. I'd much rather be by myself, but I need to remember to be part of a group.

I'm from the Marten clan. In our tribe, your clan identity is how you learn your responsibilities in life. Each clan has a place in the lodge. The Marten clan is at the western door. Our role within the tribe is to protect the people. I've been very blessed because I've been able to fulfill my clan responsibilities by vocationally working with chemical dependency for many years and now HIV.

Part of what I do at the Minnesota American Indian AIDS Task Force is deal a lot with young people and issues of identity. Who are you? Where do you come from? Who are your people? With a life-threatening illness, we're the first step to finding your place and become reconnected with the community.

I know who I am today. I didn't know when my kids were young. I remember clearly the first time I ever saw women that I could identify as lesbians. I was 16 and working nights as a waitress in a steakhouse. They came in during the bar rush. Two of them were really fem and the other two were butch and identical twins. They had on slim-cut Nehru jackets and Beatle boots. Some of the men started in on the fems with, "Can't you get anything better than that?" I remember being outraged and wondered why somebody didn't say something and tell these guys to shut up!

That was the first time in my life I could identify with lesbians. In the Native culture, it's very difficult because all Native women look the same. In a lot of tribes like mine, there are no gender-specific roles, so how the hell do you know? At least with this generation, the kids can see and identify. If people share with them, then they'll know they have a choice.

When we were growing up in northern Minnesota and my parents would go to town, my brother Michael and I would get dressed up in their clothes. He would put on my mother's clothes and I would put on my father's. I would be Elvis and he would be Diana Ross and all our younger sisters would be the Supremes. My brother and I got kind of warped because we used to walk to town and see every Rock Hudson and Doris Day movie ever made for 20 cents.

I raised my kids as a single mother. My oldest daughter Suzie was born in 1969. My whole life

> " I have a ceremonial name, *Nagahmoo Mahengin*, which translates into 'Singing Wolf.' When I think about my name, it gives me something to aspire to — to take care of the young, to care for the elderly, to be a social creature. "

changed at that point. I had done very well in school and got a scholarship to a private school. I got pregnant in the spring of 1968 in my senior year. I did graduate, but I did not go to college. Instead, I took care of my daughter. Her father and I never married. I never told him that I was pregnant, that was my choice.

Suzie was about a year and a half when I met my ex-husband. We met and got married and had my second daughter Melissa in 1971. We were married for about two years and then divorced.

This sounds so stereotypical, but when they were born, my life changed totally. All of a sudden you're responsible for this little person, and it's an overwhelming feeling. My oldest daughter Suzie is deaf in one ear. I remember when we found out that there wasn't anything that they could do about it. She was six when she went through all the tests. I remember being so angry that day. They can build all these bombs, but they can't figure out what to do with kids with disabilities.

My greatest challenge as a mother was dealing with racism and the economics of raising two children. When my kids were small, I worked. I went to school nights. I went to an AA meeting one night a week. There was no time and everything had to happen according to schedule. First thing Saturday morning we hauled our clothes to the laundromat, then we walked to the grocery store. If those things didn't happen on Saturday, everything was off-kilter.

They always had the basics, but there was never enough time to spend with them. I never got to take them to the circus. Entertainment was popcorn, penny poker and rollerskating.

I have two parenting experiences: I have my girls, my daughters; and I've been raising my oldest grandson, Kirby. He's lived with me since he was born. Some of my views on parenting have changed over the years. I'm older and wiser. I think it's really important to be open to young people about who you are. Kirby has always known that grandma is a lesbian. All of my grandchildren know that. All of my nieces and nephews know. They know they have choices. It's not that heterosexuality is superior to being gay or lesbian. Their lives are much richer. They have a whole different range of human experiences to draw from, just from being around different kinds of people.

> **This sounds so stereotypical, but when they were born, my life changed totally. All of a sudden you're responsible for this little person, and it's an overwhelming feeling.**

ACKNOWLEDGEMENTS

This book was made possible through the collaborative effort, support and vision of many people. Most importantly, I would like to thank my life partner, Diana Herrera. Without her dedication, patience, intuition and creativity, this book would never have come to life.

Through our fundraising efforts, we received substantial and sustaining loans from seven women philanthropists. Without their financial support and trust in our vision, this project would never have manifested. Our heartfelt thanks to: Marta Drury, Cindy Ewing, Janie Oakes, Catherine Carhart and Ann Hollingsworth, Jody Cole and Tracey Lake.

We would like to acknowledge and thank all those who made financial contributions to this project: John and Alice Seyda, Mary Lee Rhodes, Kristie Graham, Gay Block and Malka Drucker, Laurie Emerich and the Funding Exchange, Lawrence Herrera and Sonia Epperson, Joy Tomchin, Tashe Kurland and Terri Grover, Sara Wiener and Joanne Richter, John and Shannon Seyda, Amy Fitzpatrick, Elizabeth Cheatham, Nedra DiFillippo and Justina Trott, Tanya Fuad, Gail Fuad, Kathy Peterman, Sherie Land and Katrin Smithback, Lisa Schrag, Pam Erickson and the American Express Foundation.

As we traveled across the country, we slept on couches, futons and guest beds. Many people took us to dinner or gave us gas money. For all in-kind donations and those who generously supported us by making our journey safe and enjoyable, we thank: Teresa Duty and Janine Aiello, Lisa Schneider and Suzie Bemis, Vickie Starr and Linda Villarosa, Vivian Larsen and Helen Kalcsitz, Susan Laeng, Alix Bjorkland and Cindy O'Rouke, Gina Sandoval and Carol Lane, Jennifer Gunnell, Antonieta Gimeno, James Seyda, Beth Seyda and Mark Tachman, John and Shannon Seyda, Sara Wiener and Joanne Richter, Nancy Tafralian and Kay Fuller, Mary Hocks and Eileen Kelly, Carol Safer, Nancy Powell, Stephanie Marciel of Creative Copy, Patty and Jim Peterson, Linda Schneider, Amy Gaudia and Troyleen Brown, Carole Bennett, Rose Yniquez, Greg and Lorraine Tornga, Marty and Priscilla Herrera, the Centners, the Trimbles, the Alfaros, and Sylvia and the Dougi clan.

Many thanks to Char Zack, our accountant who donated her services and time, Diane Hall, who joyously took on the role of unpaid financial advisor, Diane Rapaport for technical and legal advice, and my sister Beth Seyda, who was the marketing wizard long before the book became a reality. We would like to thank my brother John, who assisted in the creation of the initial proposal and gave critical feedback on all negotiations and financial decision; my brother Tim, who gave artistic and financial advice; and my brother James, who made us laugh and kept us inspired. Many thanks to our parents, John and Alice Seyda and Alice Herrera, for giving us invaluable love, time, creative and financial support throughout. Many thanks to my sister Mary Jean Seyda and her

partner Maggie for keeping us focused and brave. To all of the Seydas and Herreras for staying behind us, including our twenty-five nieces and nephews.

Our profound gratitude to photographer Barbara Van Cleve who put us in touch with philanthropists in Santa Fe and gave us the jumpstart we needed, and to photojournalist, Donna Ferrato for her immediate enthusiasm and for sending the work to Verve Editions. We gratefully acknowledge and appreciate all of the hard work and dedication of Gary Chassman of Verve Editions for taking this project under his wing and finding the perfect home for it. Thanks to Melinda Meyer for her assistance in running the Verve production office. Many thanks to Carol Judy Leslie of Bulfinch Press for recognizing the work's artistic and historic significance, our editor Karen Dane, Amy Rhodes, Josh Marwell, Jennifer Marshall and the entire sales and marketing team at Little, Brown and Company for their enthusiasm and support.

For the beauty and impeccable design of this book, we thank art director, Julie Sullivan, project manager, P. J. Nidecker, and production assistant, Jessica Lundburg. We also thank our copy editor Euan Bear, and Roberto Capelli at Grafotitoli. Prints were made initially by Richard Jackson during the first half of our field work. The final prints for the book were made by Keith Schreiber. Thank you, Keith, for producing brilliant and luminous prints.

A sincere thank you to all of the people throughout the country who contributed in many special ways: Randy Burns, the National Center for Lesbian Rights, Lee Lovinfosse, Nubia and Dredlite, Debra Olinger, Kathleen Donahue, Jamie Smith, Diana Berg, Dipti Ghosh, *Trikone*, Doreena Wong of the Asian & Pacific Islander Lesbian and Bisexual Network, Pat McKenna, Toria Price, Stefan Lynch and Felicia Park-Rogers of Children of Lesbians and Gays Everywhere, Karen Morrison, editor for *Rubyfruit Journal,* Canyon Sam, Colette Barajas, Col. Margarethe Cammermeyer, Dr. Susan Love, Navahine, Tim Fisher and Ray Drew of the Gay and Lesbian Parents Coalition International, Diane Anderson and Heather Findlay of *Girlfriends* Magazine, Roger Montoya and Seal Ballinger, Darrell Wilson, Sharon Lim-Hing, Beth Goldberg at SF CameraWork, David Monson, Karen Riedell of the *Red Rock News,* Bill Hayes, Laura Lent, the Exhibitions and Programming Manager of the San Francisco Public Library, Paula DiDonato, Cheri Pies, Kerri Pickett, Terry Bogus and CenterKids, Karen Kahn and Linda Wong of *Sojourner,* Marissa Gonzales, *Just Out* Magazine, Nancy Kosciolek, Carol Lilygren, Arlis Arnold, Emily Gonzales and Pat McKenna.

Thanks to our homegirls and sisters in spirit: Teresa Duty, for providing us with food, friends, the land, music and humor; Deborah Wozniak, for her astute eye and precise feedback, heartwarming conversations and postcards; Sydne Mahoné, wisdomkeeper, poet and friend, thank you for many illuminating moments, insight, faith and maintaining the dream.